TURNING POINTS

I0867090

By Therese Harasymiw

THE INDUSTRIAL REVOLUTION

Cavendish Square
New York

Published in 2022 by Cavendish Square Publishing, LLC 29 E. 21st Street
New York, NY 10010

Copyright © 2022 by Cavendish Square Publishing, LLC

First Edition

No part of this publication may be reproduced, stored in a retrieval system, or transmitted in any form or by any means—electronic, mechanical, photocopying, recording, or otherwise—without the prior permission of the copyright owner. Request for permission should be addressed to Permissions, Cavendish Square Publishing, 29 E. 21st Street
New York, NY 10010. Tel (877) 980-4450; fax (877) 980-4454.

Website: cavendishsq.com

This publication represents the opinions and views of the author based on his or her personal experience, knowledge, and research. The information in this book serves as a general guide only. The author and publisher have used their best efforts in preparing this book and disclaim liability rising directly or indirectly from the use and application of this book.

Portions of this work were originally authored by Kevin Hillstrom and published as *The Industrial Revolution* (*American History*). All new material this edition authored by Therese Harasymiw.

All websites were available and accurate when this book was sent to press.

Library of Congress Cataloging-in-Publication Data

Names: Harasymiw, Therese, author.
Title: The industrial revolution / Therese Harasymiw.
Description: New York : Cavendish Square Publishing, [2022] | Series:
Turning points | Includes bibliographical references and index.
Identifiers: LCCN 2020053553 | ISBN 9781502660909 (library binding) | ISBN
9781502660893 (paperback) | ISBN 9781502660916 (ebook)
Subjects: LCSH: Industrial revolution–Juvenile literature. | Economic
history–Juvenile literature.
Classification: LCC HD2321 .H27 2022 | DDC 909.81–dc23
LC record available at https://lccn.loc.gov/2020053553

Editor: Therese Harasymiw
Copy Editor: Abby Young
Designer: Deanna Paternostro

Some of the images in this book illustrate individuals who are models. The depictions do not imply actual situations or events.

CPSIA compliance information: Batch #CS22CSQ: For further information contact Cavendish Square Publishing LLC, New York, New York at 1-877-980-4450.

Printed in the United States of America

Find us on

TABLE OF CONTENTS

A REVOLUTION OF INNOVATION

When people think of a revolution, they often think of government upheaval, but a revolution can also mean far-reaching changes in other realms of society. That is why the period of time called the Industrial Revolution was so named. It was a true revolution of industry. Not only was it a time of great change in the technology of industry, but those changes affected nearly every aspect of Western culture. In about a century's time, the Industrial Revolution brought about innumerable inventions and modifications in machinery, tools, and the processes of manufacturing, as well as new sources of energy and forms of business and trade. The combined impact of these innovations laid the foundation for modern life. In the process, the Age of Industrialization, as the period is sometimes called, brought the United States—home to the most impressive successes of the time—to its position as one of the foremost superpowers in the world.

However, the Industrial Revolution did not begin in the United States. It sparked first in Great Britain in the late 1700s. Prior to that time, production of goods was dependent on the power of physical labor from humans and animals. When machines powered by water, steam, and fossil fuels were introduced, they provided an efficient

Great Britain was the birthplace of the Industrial Revolution. In this photograph from the late 1800s, women pose with machinery in Smith's Woolcombing Works in Yorkshire, England.

alternative to traditional, slower means of production. While the revolution in manufacturing spread to other European countries in the early 19th century, its impact was felt most strongly across the Atlantic Ocean, in the United States. The United States had ambitious immigrants, a capitalist economy, and plentiful natural resources. Combined, these elements helped change the makeup of the nation from a largely agricultural society to one dominated by industry in just a few decades. The country's economic and cultural focus shifted from farms to cities that had been small villages just years before. American life changed permanently.

New Machines, New Jobs

Textiles are fabrics, such as cotton and wool, or the materials used to make fabrics. Before machines were introduced to the textile industry, textiles were produced and sold through what is known as a cottage industry. This means clothing was made and sold quite literally in people's cottages, or homes. However, during the Industrial Revolution, machinery took textiles out of people's hands and into a factory setting. This was the first major industry affected by

This painting shows the Wason Manufacturing Company, which produced railroad cars, in 1880. Railroad cars were essential in the transportation of people and goods during the Industrial Revolution and beyond.

the Industrial Revolution, and in the United States, it began in the textile mills of New England. These same mills were the first American businesses to introduce the "factory system" of mass production. Under this system, workers and large machines were brought together in one space, and workers were responsible for specialized jobs in the production process. This type of manufacturing quickly spread to other industries.

As the 1800s marched on, technological breakthroughs, new methods of distribution, and the ambitions of wealthy investors brought about a wave of new industries. Railroads and steamships chugged across the American landscape, giving farmers, ranchers, manufacturers, and retailers access to markets that lay hundreds of miles away. Steel foundries and oil refineries roared to life, providing energy for the operation of massive factories and essential materials for the growing cities those factories inhabited.

Transformation and Turmoil

As scholar Peter Stearns observed, "The industrial revolution constituted one of those rare occasions in world history when the human species altered its framework of existence."[1] Certainly, it had an astonishing economic impact. The unparalleled levels of production in manufacturing and commercial agriculture strengthened the American economy. This resulted in greater wealth and a larger population in the United States. Even life expectancy rose. The economic impact of the Industrial Revolution was fully matched by its influence on American culture and identity. The economic opportunities found in factories and mills convinced millions of immigrants from Europe and other parts of the world to make a new home in the United States. The inventors and engineers that the revolution inspired brought electrical lighting, indoor plumbing, and other new comforts and conveniences to American families. The Industrial Revolution also gave Americans the means to discover—through travel or newspapers—distant parts of the country that would have otherwise remained mysteries. The inventions of the steamship and the locomotive helped open the West, which the United States would eventually settle, extending its borders all the way to the Pacific Ocean. The Age of Industrialization changed the United States' relationship with the rest of the world too. It transformed the country into a formidable military power and the leading source of wheat, cotton, coal, oil, and other vital goods by the early 20th century.

However, the Industrial Revolution also could not cover up—and indeed, caused—massive social and economic turmoil in the United States. The population boom that it brought to cities meant overcrowded conditions. To boost profits, factory owners were guilty of paying their workers low salaries for long hours in hazardous conditions. Young children were also forced to work under these circumstances. Racial divisions and discrimination were apparent as people clamored for industrial jobs.

Finally, the role of slavery in the Industrial Revolution cannot be denied. The mechanization of cotton production gave the South a powerful incentive to keep Black Americans enslaved. Without enslaved people to work in the cotton fields, the machines that made cotton the most profitable crop in the world would lie idle, and the Southern economy would fall apart—or so enslavers argued. It was an argument that would continue until the American Civil War ripped across the nation from 1861 to 1865.

The Price of Industry?

Not everyone supported all of the innovations of the Industrial Revolution. Some felt the products that came out of the factories lacked the beauty and craftsmanship of the man-made pieces. Others railed against the machinery that was seemingly taking their place in the world. In fact, by the end of the 1800s, some Americans felt the fast-paced world in which they now lived was ruining the nation's vitality and moral character. "A sense of injustice … had become part of the new glittering, gaudy machine age," wrote one critic. "Machines of steel and copper and wood and stone, and bookkeeping and managerial talent, were creating a new order. It looked glamorous. It seemed permanent; yet … discontent rose in the hearts of the people."[2]

As time moved on, people also came to recognize the negative impact that the burning of fossil fuels was having on the industrialized world. These energy sources, especially coal and oil, had helped power manufacturing. The burning of nonrenewable resources like these would later be understood to contribute to problems plaguing our planet today, such as air pollution and climate change. Additionally, large areas of wilderness were sacrificed to the mining companies, railroads, and logging corporations that dominated the American economy, changing the natural landscape forever in the name of progress.

Efforts to address the dissatisfaction surrounding issues connected to the Industrial Revolution took many forms, from social reform movements to increased government regulation. However, significant groups in the American public—especially those who were thriving in the new economy—opposed these measures as anti-business or un-American. Battles about some of these concerns continue to rage to this day.

The Revolution Continues

Undeniably, the economic, social, and entrepreneurial forces unleashed by the Industrial Revolution continue to shape the course of American lives. Although the Industrial Revolution is often said to have ended around the mid-1800s, there is no clear end date. In fact, some say it continued on or, at least, paved the way for more periods of growth in industry and innovation. Some call the late 1800s and early 1900s the Second Industrial Revolution. It was characterized by the growth of railroads, the spread of telegraph and then telephone communication, the rise of steel in construction, and the introduction of inventions made possible by the internal combustion engine, including the automobile and airplane. This period, in turn, ushered in the age of computers and digital technology that we live in today.

While modern inventions such as the internet and smartphones may seem vastly more sophisticated than the tools of the Industrial Age, they are inextricably linked. None of these technological achievements would have come about if it had not been for the ambitious inventors and bold entrepreneurs who first brought the Industrial Revolution to life.

CHAPTER ONE

BRITAIN SETS THE STAGE

Many historians have pinpointed the year 1793 as the beginning of the Industrial Revolution in the United States. That was the year a British immigrant named Samuel Slater opened a textile mill in Rhode Island. Slater could not have opened that mill, touching off the U.S. Industrial Age, without the prior advances of British innovators, though. In fact, he copied British machinery designs.

The Industrial Revolution had been changing life in Great Britain for several decades before Slater launched his historic enterprise, especially in the textile industry. However, the British did their best to keep their inventions and processes on their island for a time. Nevertheless, the knowledge gradually found its way to other nations.

Of the many noteworthy British inventions of the era, perhaps the most significant to industry was the improved practical steam engine, the work of Scottish inventor James Watt. Machinery run by this steam engine took the place of simpler machines powered by water, wind, animals, and people. In turn, factories using large steam engines increasingly took the place of small workshops and home-centered businesses. Watt's invention was just one of many innovations that would transform Great Britain, the United States, and other parts of the world.

The spinning jenny, first developed in the 1700s, was hand-powered. The driving wheel was turned with the right hand, causing the spindles to rotate, while the draw bar, controlling the drafting of the threads, was operated with the left hand.

The Birth of the Modern Textile Industry

Great Britain, which includes the countries of England, Wales, and Scotland, is located off the northern coast of western Europe. This region provided an ideal foundation for the birth of the Industrial Revolution. The country had a stable government, a thriving agricultural economy, a sophisticated banking system, and a culture that encouraged business enterprise. England itself was sometimes described as a nation of shopkeepers, and this was meant as a compliment. It was also a nation of investors, which proved to be a critical element in the early days of industrialization. Wealthy British investors at the time were keenly interested in new business opportunities. In the mid-1700s, a series of events in the nation's modest textile industry caught their eye.

The British textile industry had long been a home-based endeavor in which individual workers took small amounts of fabrics to their homes or shops; created garments, blankets, and other goods; and returned the finished product to a business or buyer in exchange for payment. Most of the textiles created under this system were made from wool rather than cotton. Cotton was viewed as a luxury fabric because the natural twist in its fibers made it very time-consuming and difficult to produce. Wool was much easier to obtain and work with at the time.

In 1733, John Kay introduced the first significant innovation in the production of textiles. Kay's flying shuttle greatly increased the speed at which cotton thread could be woven into cloth on a loom. This milestone was followed three decades later by the introduction of the spinning jenny, created by James Hargreaves. Wigmaker Richard Arkwright invented the spinning frame, which was particularly important because it gave textile makers the first automated process for spinning cotton yarn. With Arkwright's invention, quality clothing and other textiles could be made quickly and inexpensively with cotton, which became more popular with manufacturers and consumers.

Arkwright's spinning frame became known as the water frame after Arkwright adjusted his product so that it could be powered by water rather than by hand. This invention made Arkwright exceedingly wealthy. In 1771, with the financial backing of numerous

HISTORY HAPPENED HERE: CROMFORD MILL

Richard Arkwright built the first water-powered cotton spinning mill on the banks of the Derwent River in Cromford, Derbyshire, England. Arkwright chose this spot in part because of a nearby lead mine. The mill used drainage water from the mine, as well as water from the Bonsall Brook, to power its water wheel.

Arkwright patented his water frame in 1769, and his first textile factory opened in 1771, becoming an instant success. Workers, mostly women and children, labored long hours to keep the factory running 24 hours a day. A single water frame was capable of winding cotton thread about 91 spools at a time. Arkwright continued to construct more mills and warehouses on the Derwent River until around 1790.

Textile production at Cromford Mill had waned by the 1830s. The buildings were used for other purposes, including laundries, cheese storage, and a brewery. In 1922, the mill was used primarily to produce pigments for paints and dyes. When the Cromford Colour Works shut down in 1979, much of the site was contaminated by the deadly chemical lead chromate. The site was purchased by the Arkwright Society, and restoration began. Today, the Derwent Valley Mills is a UNESCO World Heritage Site that includes tours, shops, and cafés.

investors, Arkwright built a massive cotton mill in Derbyshire and later established several other water-powered textile mills. These operations are widely regarded as early examples of the modern industrial factory system.

The British Textile Boom

The industrial changes in textile manufacturing predicated by the spinning jenny, water frame, and power loom (invented by

This drawing shows workers in a British cotton mill operating power looms, one of the inventions that took cotton cloth manufacturing out of the home and into the factory.

Edmund Cartwright in 1785) convinced numerous investors to become involved in the industry. Many areas of Great Britain, such as the county of Lancashire, experienced a boom of textile factory construction during the 1770s and 1780s, especially along rivers that could turn the waterwheels of the new mill designs. Once these factories were built, orders for textile products piled up, and factory owners became wealthy. "Cotton cloth production increased dramatically," confirmed economic historian John Steele Gordon. "In 1765 about five hundred thousand pounds of cotton was spun into thread in Britain, almost all of it at home. Twenty years later sixteen million pounds were spun, mostly in factories."[1]

It soon became clear that textile production in Britain was becoming a booming industry. Public demand for inexpensive cotton clothing and other materials continued to rise in the early 1800s. The industry was able to meet this demand because it could draw on the large cotton crops generated in India, which was a British colony at the time. Once cotton production in the United States began to flourish in the 1790s, thanks to Eli Whitney's cotton gin, British textile factories had another large source of cotton. In addition, Britain had large reserves of coal, so when the steam engine replaced water power in the early 1800s, the country's textile makers were able to maintain a high level of production.

In 1781, Arkwright opened the first steam-powered textile mill in Manchester. By the turn of the 19th century, Manchester as well

Manchester, England, quickly became an essential hub in the cotton industry in the early 19th century. Cotton factories sprang up quickly. This helped Manchester become "Cottonopolis," but the city also became known for the pollution caused by the new factories.

as other British cities had become the world's leading centers for the manufacturing of textiles. Manchester acquired the nickname "Cottonopolis," a tribute to its importance to the global cotton trade. In the process, British textile centers also became the first cities in the world to experience the dark side of industrial mass production.

While the booming textile industry was beneficial in many ways, most mill owners in Great Britain exploited the workforce in their quest for riches. Arkwright and other mill owners employed mostly women and children, some as young as 11 years old. The mills ran nonstop, and shifts could be as long at 12 hours. In addition, working conditions were usually dangerous. and injuries were common. One Manchester physician, J. P. Kay, expressed outright horror at the situation. "Whilst the engine runs, the people must work—men, women and children are yoked together with iron and steam," he described. "[People are] chained fast to the iron machine, which knows no suffering and no weariness."[2] Other observers noted that the rapid increase in textile factories had changed huge areas of the British countryside. The mills were considered eyesores, and waste material piled up outside the factories.

Such complaints did not convince factory owners or government officials to address the problems of industrial pollution, child labor, or worker exploitation. They did, however, bring about the first social reform movements dedicated to improving working conditions and making factories safe places to work.

The Rise of Steam

Early experiments in steam power occurred in Europe as far back as the 1600s. Not much came of these efforts, though, until 1705, when a British blacksmith named Thomas Newcomen produced a

James Watt did not stop tinkering with his steam engine after its early success. This engine, developed in the late 1770s, was notable for its gears, which were sometimes described as "sun and planet gears."

primitive engine that was powered by steam. Within a few decades, steam-powered pumps based on Newcomen's design were being used widely to remove water from British coal-mining pits. In 1765, Scottish inventor James Watt unveiled a new steam engine that could be used for a range of industrial purposes. Watt's invention marked the end of the long quest by European inventors to harness steam for human use.

Watt's steam engine design was based on Newcomen's engine, but it was far more efficient and sophisticated. Most importantly, it could be easily modified for use in the textile mills located across Britain. Existing mills that invested in the new steam technology were able to expand their production capacity dramatically. The arrival of Watt's steam engine, which was fueled by coal, freed mill owners from having to build their facilities on the banks of rivers and streams. Textile factories could now be erected in regions of Great Britain far from any river current.

The rise of steam technology sparked economic growth and innovation in other industries across Great Britain. In British ironworks, for example, the introduction of steam-powered bellows in blast furnaces helped iron makers switch from charcoal to coke, an inexpensive by-product of coal. Burning coke in ironworks furnaces generated higher temperatures than burning charcoal. This allowed ironmasters to burn off a greater amount of imperfections and produce iron products of greater strength and durability.

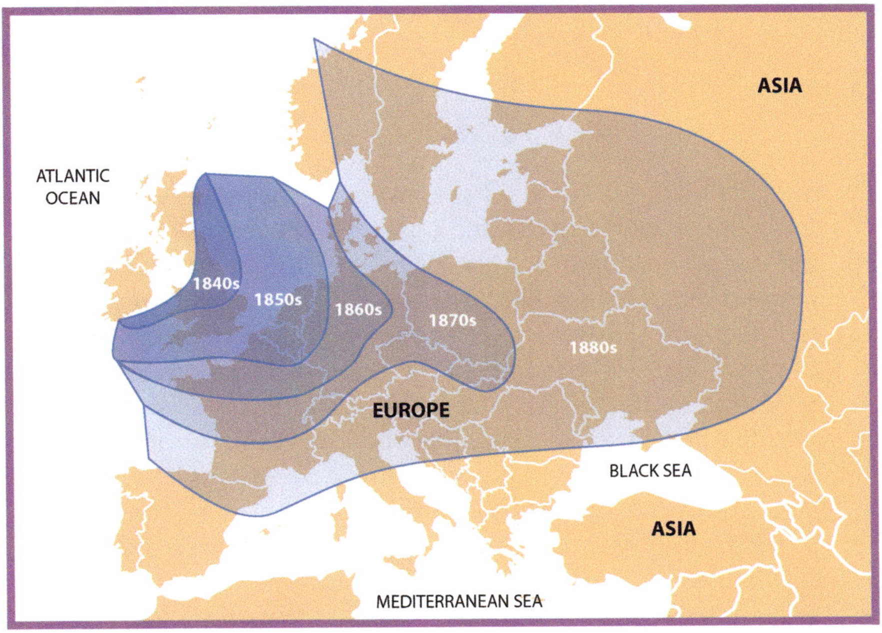

This map shows approximately when the key ideas of the Industrial Revolution spread throughout Europe.

Similar to textile factories, steam power freed flour mills from England to Wales from the necessity of building and operating next to waterways. Perhaps most significant, steam engines became the centerpiece of efforts to make an exciting new mode of transportation—the railroad—more efficient and effective. By the 1820s, steam-powered railways were emerging as an important method of transporting coal—the fuel of industrialization—and other goods to cities and factories in Britain. Steam power helped Britain transition from a home-based economy to a machine-powered one. This transition spread to other European countries and the United States.

Whitney's Cotton Gin

The advent of the Industrial Revolution in Britain coincided with momentous events unfolding across the Atlantic Ocean in North America. England lost its American colonies after the American Revolution. These colonies became the United States of America. The successful rebellion that resulted in the establishment of the United

PAST MEETS PRESENT: STEAM POWER

In the first century CE, Greek inventor Heron of Alexandria (also known as Hero) created a steam-driven device that was more of a toy than an engine. He called it the aeolipile. Heron made a metal sphere held in place by two hollow tubes that fed steam into the sphere. The sphere also had two tubes that allowed steam to escape. The escaping steam caused the sphere to rotate. While Heron's device was just a novelty, it was the first steam turbine. The aeolipile demonstrated that steam could be used to power man-made devices.

In 1698, British engineer and inventor Thomas Savery patented the first steam engine, used to pump water out of coal mines. Several inventors improved on Savery's steam engine, including James Watt. Watt's contributions to steam technology helped lead to early power plants. Englishman Richard Trevithick built the first steam locomotive in 1803, and American inventor Robert Fulton introduced the first successful passenger steamboat in 1807.

Today, we use fossil fuels and other, more sustainable resources to power trains, ships, aircraft, and much more. However, steam power still plays an important role in many electrical power plants all over the world. Power plants use coal, gas, nuclear energy, or solar power to heat water to make steam. The steam is used to make giant turbines spin, giving rotational power to large electrical generators.

This is a 19th-century drawing of what Heron's early aeolipile might have looked like.

States angered the British people. It did not, however, blind them to the potential economic benefits of trade with their former subjects, especially after a young American inventor named Eli Whitney invented a machine in 1793 that revolutionized the textile industry once again. Whitney's cotton gin (short for "engine") solved the challenge of separating cotton's fibers from its seeds.

"The machine was simplicity itself," wrote scholar John Steele Gordon of Whitney's cotton gin. He added:

> *Whitney studded a roller with nails, set half an inch apart. When the roller was turned, the nails passed through a grid, pulling the cotton lint from below through the grid, but leaving the seeds behind. A rotating brush swept the lint off the nails into a compartment while the seeds fell into a separate compartment. With Whitney's cotton gin, a laborer could do in a single day what had taken twenty-five laborers to do in that amount of time before.*[3]

In just a few years, the impact of Whitney's invention could be seen throughout the South. Before the cotton gin, the United States had produced less than one percent of the world's total cotton crop. By the first decade of the 19th century, however, the cotton gin had enabled the nation to compete in the world market. U.S.

Southern farmers did not want to pay Whitney to service their cotton gins, so they built their own. This nearly ruined Whitney financially. Eventually, several state governments paid Whitney for his contribution to the agriculture industry. A drawing of a cotton gin is shown here.

FROM THE SOURCE: A LETTER FROM ELI WHITNEY

In 1793, Eli Whitney traveled to Savannah, Georgia. In August, he wrote a letter to his father telling him about his experiences and his invention:

> *During this time I heard much said of the extreme difficulty in ginning Cotton, that is, separating it from its seeds. There were a number of very respectable Gentlemen at Mrs. Greene's who all agreed that if a machine could be invented which would clean the cotton with expedition, it would be a great thing both to the Country and to the inventor . . . In about ten Days I made a little model, for which I was offered, if I would give up all right and title to it, a Hundred Guineas. I concluded to relinquish my school and turn my attention to perfecting the Machine. I made one before I came away which required the labor of one man to turn it and with which one man will clean ten times as much cotton as he can in any other way before known and also cleanse it much better than in the usual mode. This machine may be turned by water or with a horse, with the greatest ease, and one [man] and a horse will do more than fifty men with the old machine. It makes the labor fifty times less, without throwing any class of People out of business. I returned to the Northward for the purpose of having a machine made on a large scale and obtaining a patent for the invention.*[1]

1. Eli Whitney, "Letter from Eli Whitney, Jr. to His Father Regarding His Invention of the Cotton Gin, 11 September 1793," Teaching American History in South Carolina Project, https://digital.scetv.org/teachingAmerhistory/tTrove/Whitney11Sept1793.htm (accessed September 29, 2020).

cotton production continued to surge in the early 1800s, and by 1830, the country was producing unprecedented levels. Factories in British textile centers fought to acquire all the cotton the American Southern states could grow.

Tragically, cotton's high demand breathed new life into slavery, which had been fading, both in importance and in practice, across

This image shows enslaved people in the United States using a variation of Eli Whitney's cotton gin. They are portrayed as happily working despite being enslaved, which was a common theme of the time.

most of America for much of the late 18th century. Abolition had been gaining traction in the agricultural South, with the aid of declining crop profits. However, the increasing profitability of cotton after the gin's invention led to a resurgence in the demand for enslaved labor—and an increasing divide between the North and South. Southern plantation owners speculated that people in the North would never try to forcibly end slavery in America due to the economic prevalence of the Southern cotton industry. "The slave-holding South is now the controlling power of the world," declared South Carolina senator James Hammond in 1858. "No power on earth dares … to make war on cotton. Cotton is king."[4]

Across the Atlantic Ocean, observers in England watched the growing tensions between the North and South in America with unease. British textile factories were so dependent on American cotton that they became alarmed at the thought of the end of slavery in the United States. They worried that, should war erupt in the United States over the issue of slavery, their textile factories would fail and many British people would go hungry from lack of work.

Industrialization Immigrates to America

By the start of the 19th century, Britain's textile centers and other mechanized industries had become the envy of the world.

THEY MADE HISTORY: SAMUEL SLATER

Samuel Slater was born in Derbyshire, England, on June 9, 1768. He was the son of a farmer but began an apprenticeship at a cotton mill when he was 14 years old. Over the next eight years, he became familiar with the mill machines, which were designed by Richard Arkwright. In 1789, Slater immigrated to the United States, secretly taking his knowledge of the machinery and processes of the successful factory with him.

With the aid of a Quaker merchant named Moses Brown, Slater built the first water-powered cotton spinning mill in the United States in Pawtucket, Rhode Island, in the early 1790s. At first, workers walked on a treadmill to generate power to run the machines. However, a waterwheel later replaced the treadmill.

Besides his use of British-designed machines, Slater also found success by dividing labor among his workers. Children as young as four years old were hired to perform the simplest tasks. Entire families both lived and worked at the mill site. Slater died in 1835 and is remembered as the "father of the American factory system."

British lawmakers tried to preserve their economic advantage over the United States and other nations by passing laws that prohibited the export of textile machinery and textile-related intellectual property. Intellectual property, a term still used today, means "creations of the mind"—such as engineering designs, works of art, and literary works—with the potential to build economic value. By passing intellectual property laws, the British hoped to keep the economic benefits of industrialization to themselves for as long as possible.

However, these efforts were doomed to fail. American leaders were determined to build a country that was not dependent on England or any other nation for its economic health. "Long before

Eli Whitney and before the first muskets were drawn at Concord [during the American Revolution] … the eventual leaders of the new republic realized that to be self-sustaining our citizens would have to dress themselves in native cloth grown and manufactured without any reliance on foreign powers,"[5] explained American scholar Stephen Yafa. In addition, the potential for riches was simply too great to keep ambitious entrepreneurs from figuring out ways to bring moneymaking ideas to America.

In 1793, British immigrant Samuel Slater opened the first industrial textile mill in the United States after completing an apprenticeship at a textile factory in England. In his facility in Pawtucket, Rhode Island, Slater, a man with an incredible memory, duplicated the British textile operations and technology he had seen in his native country. If not the beginning of the Industrial Revolution in the United States, Slater's factory was an early milestone in American economic history.

Two decades later, in 1812, Massachusetts native Francis Cabot Lowell returned to the United States after a two-year stay in England. During his time in Manchester and other industrial cities, Lowell had committed to memory many parts of their rapidly evolving textile operations. When he returned to the United States, Lowell built textile mills in Waltham, Massachusetts, that integrated all aspects of the cotton manufacturing process—even the dyeing of cloth—under one roof. By 1820, Lowell's mills had flourished to become America's first corporate empire. The industrial factory system that had transformed Great Britain into an economic powerhouse was now firmly established in the United States.

How You See History

1. How important do you think it is to preserve and honor locations such as Cromford Mill in England and Old Slater Mill in Rhode Island?
2. Why were the first British textile factories a success?
3. Do you think the Southern cotton industry would have been as successful without British textile factories? Why or why not?

CHAPTER TWO

AMERICA TAKES THE LEAD

In just a few years, Watt's steam engine, Whitney's cotton gin, Slater and Lowell's factory systems, and other innovations began to transform American life in innumerable ways. The United States was an ideal incubator for industrial growth, thanks to several factors. First, it was home to a growing population that could fill new factories with laborers. Also, the young nation's capitalist economic system encouraged investment and growth in business. In addition, the United States had a wealth of natural resources, including rivers deep and wide enough to accommodate ships, large reserves of coal and other fuel sources, dense forests filled with wood, and acres and acres of fertile farmland. These resources gave eager, talented American engineers, inventors, and entrepreneurs the power to strengthen the Industrial Revolution in the United States.

America Embraces the Revolution

In many parts of Britain, industrialization was greeted at first with distrust and resistance. Many British people preferred their traditional way of life. They feared the impact of new machines and factories on their jobs and families. When people heard stories about the working conditions that existed in factories in Manchester and other industrial cities, public fears about industrialization became more intense. By the early

Not everyone was happy with the growth of industry. Luddites destroyed factory machinery to protest industrialization. They were said to be followers of Ned Ludd, but no evidence exists to prove he was real.

19th century, British textile workers known as Luddites had organized violent protests against the mechanized textile mills.

In the United States, however, machines, factories, and steam power were typically welcomed with open arms. Both rural farmers and city factory workers were happy to have machines that could make their work less exhausting. Factory owners gladly embraced new technology that could increase the output and efficiency of their operations. Consumers welcomed the promise of greater variety and availability of goods. Lawmakers and community leaders shared the widespread American belief that their new nation was destined for great things.

For many U.S. leaders, the Industrial Revolution was viewed as the means by which America could become a major world power. The population was quickly growing, and American society was well prepared for industrialization. Mechanization and other aspects of industrialization were instantly recognized as keys to greater wealth—the most common way of measuring success in the United States. Talented entrepreneurs and engineers—from the United States and from around the world—flocked to newly mechanized industries.

Transportation Fuels the Revolution

Early American industrialism was centered in the northeastern states, which had the highest concentrations of population in the early 1800s. The metropolitan centers of this region—such as Boston, Massachusetts; Philadelphia, Pennsylvania; and New York City—had plenty of willing workers on hand and the support of banks and other sources of investment capital.

In addition, all these cities had access to rivers, lakes, or the Atlantic Ocean. The proximity to navigable waterways was a particularly important factor in the economic and industrial prospects of an American city in the early 1800s. Rivers such as the Hudson, Connecticut, Potomac, James, and Susquehanna provided essential waterpower for New England's early textile mills. However, steam power (generated by burning coal) soon replaced waterpower in American factories, and most factories no longer needed water to power machinery. The waterways became more important as transportation routes. New York City, for example, became an early center of shipping, banking, and industry because it was built at the juncture of a deep Atlantic harbor and the Hudson River. The same resources—a deep ocean bay and a great river (the Mississippi)—accounted for the emergence of New Orleans,

Steamships in New Orleans were loaded with bales of cotton for delivery to locations around the world.

Louisiana, as the South's leading center of trade.

By the 1810s and 1820s, American lawmakers and businesspeople endeavored to make the nation's water-based transportation system even more effective by constructing massive canals. They saw the need to connect potential agricultural regions with canals to make transportation more efficient and lucrative. Man-made waterways and natural river systems accelerated the spread of industry and wealth to more areas of the country and facilitated the rise of more farmland as well as urban centers.

The Erie Canal

The most ambitious of these massive canal projects in the United States was the Erie Canal, which spanned New York State, connecting Lake Erie in the west with the Atlantic Ocean in the east. After years of pressure from supporters of the project, including DeWitt Clinton—a politician who had served New York as a U.S. senator, governor, and mayor of New York City—construction on the canal began in 1817. Clinton promised that the canal would "convey more riches on its waters than any other canal in the world," transporting resources "to be expended [spent] in great public improvements; in encouraging the arts and sciences; in patronizing the operations of industry; in fostering the inventions of genius, and in diffusing [spreading] the blessing of knowledge."[1]

In 1825, the Erie Canal's surveyors, engineers, and laborers completed their work eight years after the massive project had broken ground. The canal stretched 363 miles (584 kilometers) from the city of Albany on the Hudson River to Buffalo on the shores of Lake Erie. By traveling up the Hudson River from New York Harbor, ships could easily reach the canal in Albany. As Clinton had predicted, the canal opened a tremendously profitable trade link between eastern population centers such as New York City and the territories of the Great Lakes region. Eastbound shipments of Great Lakes timber, minerals, and crops soared.

Cities like Buffalo, Rochester, Syracuse, and Utica grew into important economic locations.

In this image, New York governor Dewitt Clinton, sometimes called the "father of the Erie Canal," pours water from Lake Erie into the Atlantic Ocean as part of the canal's opening ceremony, symbolizing how the canal connected U.S. waterways.

Meanwhile, the holds of westbound ships were loaded with factory-made textiles and farming tools intended for the migrating families who were flooding into the newly accessible farmlands of the upper Midwest. Many of these changes were evident within a few months of the canal's opening. "It is an impressive sight to gaze up and down the canal," one admirer declared. "In either direction, as far as the eye can see, long lines of boats can be observed. By night, their flickering head lamps give the impression of swarms of fireflies."[2] The Erie Canal transformed the Midwest into an agricultural powerhouse.

All over the country, investors, engineers, and lawmakers began to launch canal-building schemes of their own. None of these systems matched the Erie Canal in size and impact, but many had significant regional economic benefits. By 1850, more than 3,700 miles (5,955 km) of canals had been constructed in America. The completion of the massive Sault Ste. Marie Canals (also known as the Soo Locks) on the St. Marys River between Lake Huron and Lake Superior opened the entire Superior region for large-scale settlement, development, and commerce.

The Erie Canal was considered a man-made wonder of its time. Each of its locks, one of which is shown here in Lockport, New York, was a device to raise or lower a boat between differing water levels.

HISTORY HAPPENED HERE: LOCKPORT, NEW YORK

While the main portion of the Erie Canal was completed in 1825, engineers and workers kept improving and expanding the canal system for the next few decades. In Lockport, New York, a particularly impressive, high-tech construction took shape in the year 1849. Lockport is located near the Niagara Escarpment, a steeply sloped section of land that stretches from western New York, through southern Ontario, and into northern Michigan. Builders needed to find a way to raise the canal approximately 60 feet (18 meters). They chose the town of Lockport to carry out this engineering feat.

Builders created a series of five locks. The "Flight of Five," an engineering marvel of the era, allowed ships to go from the lower section of the canal to the higher section in very little time. Today, people can take a cruise to experience a trip on the canal and learn more about how the technology of the locks works.

Steamboats on the Move

The expansion of America's system of navigable waterways corresponded with the development of the steam-powered engine, which had revolutionized the form and function of the boats that traveled those coastal waters, rivers, and canals. In the 1780s and 1790s, American inventor John Fitch had carried out the first successful experiments with a steam-powered boat. However, it was not until 1807 that the concept of steam-powered boats and ships really caught the attention of the American public. That year, American inventor and entrepreneur Robert Fulton took his *Steamboat*, as he named it, 150 miles (240 km) up the Hudson River from New York City to Albany. He returned to New York City soon after with a ship full of paying passengers. This was the start of a lucrative steamboat business.

Other American inventors joined Fulton in improving the steamboat. The development of high-pressure steam engines was another key milestone in the development of steam travel. The first steamboat innovators in the United States had powered their boats with Watt steam

FROM THE SOURCE: "THE CANAL BOAT"

American author Nathaniel Hawthorne was an early traveler on the Erie Canal. He recorded his experiences aboard a small boat in an essay titled "The Canal Boat," first published in *New England Magazine* in 1835. Hawthorne described many sights, including workers, animals, bridges, rural scenery, and burgeoning cities. Hawthorne's trip on the young Erie Canal inspired others to make the journey themselves and see the beauty of New York State, as well as the fruits of the Industrial Revolution. Here is an excerpt from his essay:

> *Two or three miles further would bring us to a lock, where the slight impediment to navigation had created a little mart of trade . . . The next scene might be the dwellinghouses and stores of a thriving village, built of wood or small gray stones, a church-spire rising in the midst, and generally two taverns . . . Passing on, we glide now into the unquiet heart of an inland city—of Utica, for instance—and find ourselves amid piles of brick, crowded docks and quays, rich warehouses and a busy population . . . Onward, also, go we, till the hum and bustle of struggling enterprise die away behind us, and we are threading an avenue of the ancient woods again.*[1]

1. Quoted in "The Canal Boat: Nathaniel Hawthorne Travels the Erie Canal," History Matters: The U.S. Survey Course on the Web, historymatters.gmu.edu/d/6212/ (accessed September 30, 2020).

engines. However, these engines were not strong enough to power boats along large rivers with strong currents. In the opening years of the 19th century, Pennsylvania inventor Oliver Evans and Richard Trevithick of Wales—each working independently—developed a more powerful and efficient high-pressure steam engine. "The Watt engine, which had helped to spark the Industrial Revolution and was the most fundamentally important technological development since the printing press three hundred years earlier, was obsolete [outdated] after only three decades," observed scholar John Steele Gordon about these

Besides his steamship, Robert Fulton designed and built a submarine and a steam warship.

advances. "The pace of change had already begun the relentless acceleration that continues to this day."[3]

It soon became clear to the world that a transportation revolution was taking place in the United States. The new high-pressure steam engines gave steamboats the ability to go upstream even against the powerful currents of the Mississippi, Missouri, and Ohio Rivers, establishing that the country's mighty rivers were no longer one-way highways.

American waterways rapidly gained more economic importance than ever before. The Mississippi River system, for example, "provided no less than sixteen thousand miles of navigable waters that drained an area of more than a million square miles from western New York State to Montana," noted John Steele Gordon. "Much of it was the finest agricultural land on earth with almost limitless economic potential. Much of it was also rich in minerals."[4] Steam power unlocked these riches for the United States.

Steady Growth in Manufacturing

Advances in steam technology took place against the backdrop of slow but steady growth in factory operations in the United States in the first three decades of the 19th century. Most of this early industrialization continued to take place in New England. It was here that Oliver Evans—the same man who designed the influential high-pressure steam engine—developed fully automated flour-mill operations in the 1780s, with minimal human labor needed to maintain and monitor the machinery.

New England was also the region where America's first great industry, textile manufacturing, was centered. By 1830, textile factories dominated the U.S. economic landscape. Between 1820 and 1840, there was

THEY MADE HISTORY: ROBERT FULTON

Robert Fulton was born to Irish immigrants on November 14, 1765. He grew up on his family's farm in Lancaster County, Pennsylvania. The farm failed, and Fulton's father died in 1774. Robert learned to read and write at home. He became an apprentice in a jewelry shop in Philadelphia, where he learned to paint miniature portraits for lockets and rings.

Fulton traveled to London, England, in 1787 in an attempt to become a professional painter, but his work was not good enough to make a living. He grew interested in a new invention that used a steam engine to create a jet of water. It inspired Fulton to study steam engines and canal engineering. In 1796, Fulton published *A Treatise on the Improvement of Canal Navigation*, which described a system of inland waterways and bridges, as well as specialized ships for carrying cargo. In 1800, Fulton built a steam-powered submarine, the *Nautilus*, and conducted tests on the Seine River in France.

Fulton returned to the United States in 1806 with plans to develop a steamboat business. In August 1807, Fulton's *Steamboat* made the 150-mile (240 km) trek from New York City to Albany. The ship made the trip in 32 hours—far better than the four days it usually took ships with sails. Fulton began commercial trips in September 1807. In 1808, after making numerous improvements and updates to his original ship, Fulton introduced the *North River Steamboat of Clermont* (or simply the *Clermont*) to the world. Fulton died in 1815 and is remembered as one of America's greatest inventors.

Robert Fulton's *Clermont* experienced unexpected events on voyages. Sometimes sailors on other boats tried to damage its paddle wheels.

a massive surge of industrial investment along the East Coast. American lawmakers in local, state, and federal governments provided all sorts of economic aid to industrializing businesses, including tax exemptions and special arrangements to limit competition. They wanted the economy to thrive.

State governments were particularly energetic in funding and starting businesses, such as banks, and public improvements, including turnpikes, bridges, harbors, and other public works projects. Banks emerged as a major investing force in American business during this era. Some of this investment capital went into textiles, but a lot was directed to new industries, such as steam shipping, railroads, and various manufacturing areas.

By the early 1850s, American factories were producing so many innovative and useful products in such great volumes that England—the home of the Industrial Revolution—began conducting studies of the U.S. manufacturing system. These reports marveled at the speed with which small U.S. shops and mills were expanding into major employers and the enormous amount of economic activity that was taking place. They admitted it would be difficult for Britain to duplicate such success, for the United States simply had more people and natural resources.

Coal Takes Control

One of the most important natural resources that drove America's rapid industrialization was coal. The steam engines that powered factories and steamships needed fuel. As the 19th century progressed, coal increasingly replaced wood as the fuel of choice. It also became the main heating fuel for households across much of America.

The first great center of coal production was Pennsylvania, which held massive deposits of high-quality anthracite coal and lower-quality bituminous coal. During the 1820s, coal-mining activity transformed Pittsburgh from a small village into a bustling city of glass production and ironworks—both fuel-intensive industries heavily dependent on coal. By 1845, millions of tons of anthracite coal had been transported out of the hills of western Pennsylvania via steamboat and railroad to factories and households along the East Coast. Western Pennsylvania was producing more anthracite coal than the rest of the country combined by the mid-1800s, and it employed a huge portion of the total coal-mining workforce.

Anthracite coal was essential in the development of the railroad industry. It ranked as a major source of income for virtually all mid-century railroad companies, as their trains delivered coal around the country. Its importance to the iron industry also made it essential for the overall buildup of the railroad industry's infrastructure. During the 1830s and 1840s, innovative processes of smelting iron from anthracite coal enabled iron makers to dramatically expand production of high-quality, reasonably priced iron rails and other materials essential for railroads. Not surprisingly, several leading railroad companies of this era became major players in the coal industry. "Anthracite country is often called the cradle of American railroading, and with good reason," explained historian Barbara Freese. She continued:

> *The anthracite mine operators were the first Americans to use rails, and they greatly advanced the science of building railways . . . The Philadelphia and Reading Railroad, one of the nation's largest and most powerful companies, dominated the area, but there would be five railways so intermingled with the anthracite trade that coal and railroading were often considered a single industry.* [5]

Forging the Iron Industry

Some of these industrial advances might have happened sooner if U.S. iron makers were quicker to embrace certain technological innovations. In the 1820s, British iron makers had introduced the coal-fired blast furnace. These forges generated higher temperatures than charcoal, a lower-quality but easily obtainable fuel that had long been used in the industry. The higher temperatures enabled iron makers to burn off a greater percentage of carbon and thus produce iron products of superior strength and durability.

In the late 1800s, young boys were hired to work in anthracite coal mines in Pennsylvania. Photographs of children such as this helped garner support for child labor laws in the United States.

Within a few years, Great Britain's iron industry had used

this technology to move to the forefront of the world's iron producers. In fact, the nation became an exporter of iron after years of being an importer. In the United States, foundry and forge owners stubbornly maintained their loyalty to the charcoal-based production system that the British had abandoned.

The American iron industry was slow to follow the British example for two reasons. First, the U.S. government had attached heavy tariffs on iron imports from England. These taxes made American iron less expensive than British iron, so people were more likely to buy it no matter the quality. In addition, the demand for iron goods was so high across the country that forge owners did not worry about producing works of premium quality on a timely basis. They knew that virtually everything they produced—from firearms to stoves to parts for ships and locomotives—would be purchased as soon as it appeared on the market.

In the 1830s, though, U.S. iron makers began to invest in the blast-furnace technology that had been such an advantage to the British. Forge owners who made the switch from charcoal to coal were enormously successful. Their output was mostly responsible for the sharp increase of U.S. iron production during the 1840s. The changing competitive environment forced some smaller and less efficient iron makers out of business. Large corporations with impressive arrays of forges and rolling mills assumed greater prominence.

Farming Innovations

As the first half of the 19th century drew to a close, industrialization was transforming the lives—and livelihoods—of farmers who lived far from the bustling factories, railroad yards, and crowded immigrant neighborhoods of expanding cities. Farmers would never have been able to meet the needs of the rapidly growing population of the United States—or meet the growing demand for cotton and other crops overseas—if they had not embraced industrialization in their operations.

The first major technological innovation that shaped American agriculture was Eli Whitney's cotton gin. The stunning growth in demand for cotton—a labor-intensive crop—increased cotton farmers' profits exponentially. However, it also made white Southern commerce and culture more dependent on slavery than ever before. This state of affairs put the South in conflict with the North, which had developed a different economic and industrial system by the 1800s. The North-based abolitionist movement condemned slavery as morally evil, but many

PAST MEETS PRESENT: FARM TECH

In the early 1800s, about 90 percent of all Americans lived on farms. Today, just 1 percent does. So, how do Americans have enough to eat? We can thank farming technology for that. In the 19th century, one farm could feed up to five people per year. By the 1940s, a farm could feed up to 19 people. In recent years, that number is up to 155 people.

As farm technology has progressed since the Industrial Age, a smaller number of farmers are growing more food on larger tracts of lands. They could not raise crops on lands this size without motorized farm equipment, such as tractors, sprayers, harvesters, and air drills. John Deere products, which made their debut during the Industrial Revolution, are still a mainstay in the farm technology world of today. Some controversial biotechnology, such as crops genetically modified to fight disease, has allowed farmers to feed more people too. With fewer and fewer farmers in the United States, it may be up to future technologies to provide for the population.

white Southerners saw calls to end slavery as a mortal threat to their economy and way of life. Decades of tension finally boiled over in 1861 with the outbreak of the American Civil War, leading to the eventual abolition of slavery.

Other technological advances in the field of agriculture had fewer controversial side effects than the cotton gin. Farm machinery, such as John Deere's 1837 wrought-iron plow and William Pennock's 1841 grain drill, enabled farmers to sow seeds much more quickly, while threshing machines introduced in the 1830s and 1840s dramatically cut harvesting time.

To many, the single most important mechanical tool to appear on farms in the 19th century was Cyrus McCormick's mechanical reaper. McCormick's reaper, which he patented in 1834, mechanized the wheat harvesting process. Farmers once had to hire many laborers to harvest their crops with handheld tools. It was a costly, slow, and exhausting

This image shows a McCormick mechanical reaper around 1851. Models in the 1870s included a mechanism to bind the cut crop, removing yet another task for the farmer.

process. The reaper, pulled by horses, was made up of a reel to gather and push back grain, a vibrating blade to cut the grain, and a platform to carry the falling grain. It could cut more wheat in a day than six farmhands.

Despite its promising debut, farmers did not buy the McCormick reaper at first. In the 1840s, McCormick made some improvements to it and slowly found buyers. A move to the Midwest proved successful, and McCormick opened a factory in Chicago, Illinois, to mass-produce his machines. He was selling more than 4,000 a year by 1856.

McCormick's life had changed, but so had the life of the average American farmer. As historian John Steele Gordon noted, "With McCormick's reaper, one man could harvest eight acres a day, not one, and the American Middle West could become the bread basket of the world. In 1839 only eighty bushels of wheat were shipped out of the infant town of Chicago. Ten years later Chicago shipped two million."[6]

Thanks to inventors like McCormick, in just a few decades, U.S. farms had become increasingly industrialized and mechanized. More people flocked to cities to work in industrial businesses, and fewer laborers were required in the field. The Industrial Revolution was changing the very landscape of the country.

How You See History

1. How do you think canals, steamships, and other innovations began to change everyday life for Americans?
2. Can you think of other industries that have been slow to accept innovations, like the U.S. iron industry was?
3. Why do you think farmers resisted buying McCormick's reaper at first?

CHAPTER THREE

AN ECONOMIC POWER EMERGES

As the 19th century progressed, the Industrial Revolution hit its peak in the United States. Unparalleled economic growth and the acquisition of new lands to the west cemented the nation as a global power. Some say this time—after the Civil War through the beginning of the 20th century—could be called the Second Industrial Revolution, though there is no clear end to the first period of the Industrial Age. During these decades, railroads, including a transcontinental track, increasingly connected the nation, and the invention of the telegraph made communication easier across the miles. Production of crops, steel, and other goods rose to all-time highs.

The United States seemed to promise riches, opportunity, and power to all, and in fact, saw an escalation in the number of immigrants seeking just that. However, the majority of wealth rested in the hands of just a few Americans, some of whom were not above waging economic war to retain their influence and prosperity. These men had recognized the industries that would dominate the economy—especially railroads, steel, and oil—and sought to control them at all costs.

◀ This train is crossing a railway bridge during the construction of the U.S. transcontinental railroad in the mid-1800s.

Railroads Connect

The first railroads that were advanced enough for profitable commercial activity appeared in the late 1820s and early 1830s. England's first practical railroad was George Stephenson's Liverpool and Manchester Railway, which began operating in 1830. Not long after, the Baltimore and Ohio (B&O) Railroad established itself as the first successful steam-powered railroad company in the United States. Neither of these railroads—or the ones that soon followed—was based on the work of a single individual. Rather, railroads were the result of the collective efforts of many engineers and inventors who mastered different components of railroad design and operation.

Unlike canals, railroads could be built nearly anywhere, and they could operate all year in all kinds of weather. These characteristics made the railroad a tool for transporting freight from one place to another and gave travelers a speedy and comfortable transportation alternative to canals and rough roads. The advantages were clear to U.S. engineers and investors, who gathered around the new technology. In 1830, the railroad industry barely existed. One decade later, however, nearly 3,000 miles (4,828 km) of track had been laid across the United States, mostly in the East. By 1850, more than 9,000 miles (14,484 km) of railroad lines snaked across America, and by the time the Civil War erupted in 1861, more than 30,000 miles (48,280 km) of lines had been built. Most lines were in the North, which gave the Union a tremendous military advantage during the war.

Many railroad lines built in the 1840s and 1850s connected cities to other cities, but others were built to link mining facilities and timber tracts to factories and mills. Wherever they were constructed, railroads changed America's social, business, and environmental landscape in lasting ways. In some respects, their legacy was a positive one, but they also had a dark side. For example, railroads gave rural farmers, ranchers, and mining companies access to markets they never had before, but they also crushed steamboat operations that had been raking in profits in the pre-railroad era. Cities and towns blossomed along rail lines and pulsed with economic activity, but this gave railroad owners extreme power over the future of entire communities. A town could see its population explode in a short time if a rail line was built through it—but if that rail line stopped running, the population would vanish. The town would be left to pay the price.

The railroad also went a long way toward making the ever-growing United States feel like a unified country, rather than a vast collection of remote communities. However, in many regions of the country, the forces it unleashed had a destructive impact on the environment. Entire forests were carried away on the backs of railroads. Towns and cities nurtured by the railroads turned the surrounding countryside into wheat fields, grazing lands, and industrial sites.

Western Settlement

The railroad was a vital instrument of western settlement. During the first half of the 19th century, the United States used the Louisiana Purchase of 1803, the treaty that ended the Mexican-American War, and land cessions from Britain to expand its territory from the eastern banks of the Mississippi River all the way to the Pacific Ocean. Most Americans were convinced it was God's will that they tame this vast wilderness, defeat the Native American inhabitants, and use the region's natural resources to improve their own lives. The belief that Americans were fated to conquer and settle the West became known as Manifest Destiny.

The 1872 painting by John Gast called *American Progress* presents ideas behind the concept of Manifest Destiny, including the racist notion that Americans would "civilize" the West.

White settlers flooded into the West in the second half of the 19th century. Eager to make better lives

FROM THE SOURCE: THE HOMESTEAD ACT OF 1862

Of all the land distribution programs instituted to encourage western settlement, none was as important as the Homestead Act of 1862. According to the act, any U.S. citizen or immigrant who was 21 years old or the head of a family could take possession of 160 acres (65 hectares) of unsettled public land for a small fee:

> *Be it enacted by the Senate and House of Representatives of the United States of America in Congress assembled, That any person who is the head of a family, or who has arrived at the age of twenty-one years, and is a citizen of the United States, or who shall have filed his declaration of intention to become such, as required by the naturalization laws of the United States, and who has never borne arms against the United States Government or given aid and comfort to its enemies, shall, from and after the first January, eighteen hundred and sixty-three, be entitled to enter one quarter section or a less quantity of unappropriated public lands, upon which said person may have filed a preemption claim, or which may, at*

for themselves and their families, these pioneers took advantage of cheap land grants and other government programs designed to encourage settlement of the West. They established farms, mining operations, towns, and cities in places that had been Native American hunting grounds only a few years earlier. By the close of the 19th century, the vast lands between the Pacific Ocean and Mississippi River supported cities and industries that rivaled the greatest cities of the East.

The transformation of the West would never have been possible without the "iron horse," as the railroad was called in frontier communities. This transportation option had transformed the economy *the time the application is made, be subject to preemption at one dollar and twenty-five cents, or less, per acre.*[1]

Homesteaders had to live on the land for at least five years and improve it, such as by cultivating crops or building a home, to keep it. However, much of the land was unsuitable for raising crops or livestock. Timber and mining companies and cattle ranchers had used their political connections to claim the best land.

1. "Transcript of Homestead Act (1862)," Our Documents, www.ourdocuments.gov/doc.php?flash=false&doc=31&page=transcript (accessed October 2, 2020).

Visitors can tour the Palmer-Epard Cabin at the Homestead National Monument of America in Nebraska. The one-room house, measuring just 14 feet (4.3 m) by 16 feet (4.9 m), was home to homesteader George Palmer, his wife, and their 10 children.

and culture of the eastern United States in the 1830s and 1840s, and it did the same thing in the West in the second half of the century. Vast networks of railroad lines moved settlers from the East to the West and gave manufacturers and farmers the means to send their products greater distances. Railroads also increased the speed by which everything—from iron ore to information—could be delivered cross-country.

In many cases, railroad companies took an even more active role in distributing western lands than state, territorial, or federal authorities. During the construction of the first transcontinental railroad, for example, the federal government authorized the distribution of

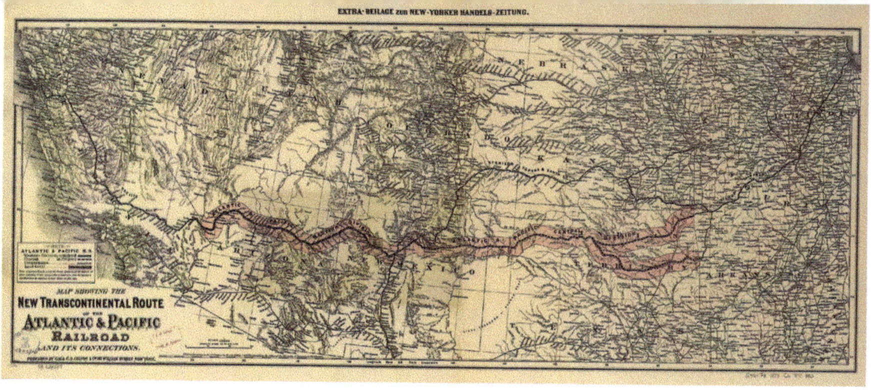

This map shows the route of a later transcontinental railroad, which helped connect areas of the American Southwest in the 1880s.

about 30 million acres (12 million ha) of public land to railroad companies along the route. The government gave up these lands to incentivize the construction of the railroad, and the Union Pacific and Central Pacific—the two companies that built it—were free to use the land for whatever purpose they wanted. Most of the time, the land was used for its natural resources, though the companies also sold it to settlers and towns looking to expand westward.

Land grant programs were essential in the settlement and development of the Great Lakes region, but they were even more important in spurring settlement in the West. Congress and various state and territorial governments granted western railroads a total of about 130 million acres (52.6 million ha) in land grants. Four railroads—the Northern Pacific; the Atchison, Topeka and Santa Fe; the Union Pacific; and the Southern Pacific—received more than half of the total land awarded. This gave the railroads a huge economic incentive to settle the West. Over time, the railroads became so closely associated with the growing American empire that many people used the language of mythology to describe the trains roaring across the countryside. Asa Whitney, who helped build the nation's first transcontinental railroad in the 1860s, declared that when traveling by train, "time & space are annihilated by steam, we pass through a City a town, [even] a country, like an arrow from Jupiters Bow."[1] In 1853, one writer described the American train as

> *the earth-shaker, the fire-breather, which tramples down the hills, which outruns the laggard [slow] winds, which leaps over the rivers, which grinds the rocks to powder and breaks down the gates*

HISTORY HAPPENED HERE: GOLDEN SPIKE NATIONAL HISTORICAL PARK

Golden Spike National Historical Park in Utah surrounds a 15-mile (24 km) length of the original transcontinental railroad created by the Union Pacific and Central Pacific Railroads. The two companies—or, more exactly, their workforces—did the incredible feat of laying about 1,800 miles (2,897 km) of track from Nebraska to California over about 6 years. This construction required blasting tunnels through mountains, building towering bridges over canyons, and other, often dangerous, tasks. The track shortened the travel time between the East and West Coasts of the United States from as long as six months to under two weeks.

At the Golden Spike National Historical Park, the place where the last spike of the transcontinental railroad—a ceremonial golden spike—was driven into the rails on May 10, 1869, is marked by a polished wooden tie. Visitors to the park today can admire replica locomotives to learn what technology was like back then and discover more about the arduous task of building the railroad.

This painting shows the celebration at the end of the construction of the transcontinental railroad. The Union Pacific built from the east, and the Central Pacific built from the west, meeting in Utah in 1869.

of the mountains . . . Shall not cities be formed from his vaporous breath, and men spring up from the cinders of his furnace?[2]

A Farming Boom

As railroad routes sprouted across the country, more land was converted for agricultural use. Not surprisingly, this expansion in land under cultivation and the arrival of mechanized farming—as well as more sophisticated use of fertilization and irrigation techniques—generated huge jumps in the agricultural industry. Between 1869 and 1899, farm production more than doubled.

Wheat production increased from 250 million bushels around 1870 to 750 million bushels in 1920, and corn production more than doubled in this same time period. Cotton production in the post–Civil War era surged as well. As the Reconstruction era gave way to discriminatory Jim Crow laws across the Deep South, white planters reasserted their power over Black sharecroppers. By the close of the 19th century, these economically penniless and politically powerless sharecroppers were helping to produce more than 10 million bales a year for the Southern cotton lords.

Investment capital and settlement patterns established manufacturing in towns and cities that had been little more than trading posts a few decades earlier. Many textile operations gradually drifted out of New England to the South, where the costs of hiring workers and shipping cotton were much lower. Meanwhile, factories and mills followed the millions of settlers who had been attracted to the West by reports of gold, promises of farmland, or steady work in timber and mining camps.

All of this economic activity and political influence turned the nation's leading railroad owners, financiers, and mining executives into wealthy and powerful men. Some of these men, such as Jay Gould, Cornelius Vanderbilt, John D. Rockefeller, and J. P. Morgan, became household names. However, fame did not translate into respect among the general public. In fact, railroad magnates and other industrial tycoons became known as "robber barons"—a negative term that reflected the belief that these men built their fortunes through ruthless exploitation of workers, cunning manipulation of lawmakers and officials, and savage attacks on competitors.

Fuel for the Revolution

The robber barons were aware of their reputation, but they paid little attention to how average Americans viewed them. Instead, they maintained their focus on advancing industrialization and increasing the riches that could be gained from it. One of their highest priorities was finding new energy sources to feed the factories, foundries, and railroads of the Industrial Revolution. Two substances—coal and oil—emerged as the precious fuels of the Industrial Age.

In colonial America, and for much of the pre–Civil War era, most of the nation's energy needs had been met by wood. Locomotives and household stoves alike were fueled in this manner. Most Americans were unaware not only of coal's superior qualities as a source of heat and energy but also of the vast tracts of coal that existed in the hills of Pennsylvania and other parts of the country. The appetite for firewood was so great, in fact, that its impact on forests was immense. The incredible rate of deforestation alarmed some Americans, who urged their fellow citizens to take better care of the wilderness. Despite this, most Americans ignored such warnings because they believed that the supply of land and resources within the nation's borders was inexhaustible.

In this political cartoon from 1883, businessmen called robber barons, including Jay Gould and Cornelius Vanderbilt, keep their businesses afloat through the hard work and low wages of their employees.

After the Civil War, though, coal consumption steadily increased. The inexpensive mineral was ideally suited for use in industrial forges, and it became the preferred energy source in many households. In the mid-1880s, coal surpassed wood as the nation's leading energy source. Virtually all of this

PAST MEETS PRESENT: ARE THERE ROBBER BARONS TODAY?

The corporate giants and financiers that the Industrial Age public named robber barons were often guilty of manipulating the economic system and laws so that they could profit. Jason "Jay" Gould, for example, organized a series of shady business deals in the 1860s and 1870s, including a bold scheme to corner the gold market in 1869. He triggered a panic on Wall Street that sent stocks plummeting. By 1881, Gould controlled a railroad empire, and his warlike attitude toward competing railways was known far and wide. When Gould died in 1892, he was regarded as one of the most hated men in America. As biographer Maury Klein wrote, "Two generations of operators, businessmen, bankers, lawyers, coupon clippers, stockholders, politicians, reformers, journalists, ministers, and other guardians of the public morals reviled him as the supreme villain of his age."[1]

Some argue that a few modern businesspeople could be considered robber barons, such as Microsoft's Bill Gates, Facebook's Mark Zuckerberg, and Amazon's Jeff Bezos. All are powerful billionaires who have been accused of eliminating rival businesses to have a monopolistic share of the marketplace. Some have been called out for allowing harmful working conditions in their factories and warehouses, just as the robber barons of the Industrial Revolution once permitted. Interestingly, in a list created by *Forbes* of the wealthiest Americans of all time, none of the modern technology moguls are as rich as the Industrial Age tycoons were (when their wealth is adjusted to reflect inflation). For example, John D. Rockefeller had a fortune worth about $336 billion today compared to Jeff Bezos's fortune of $196 billion. Truly, the Industrial Age robber barons had wealth beyond imagination.

1. Maury Klein, *The Life and Legend of Jay Gould* (Baltimore, MD: Johns Hopkins University Press, 1997), p. 3.

coal came from domestic sources, as mining companies tapped into vast deposits in Pennsylvania, West Virginia, and Ohio, as well as Colorado and other western states.

By the beginning of the 20th century, Americans from Maine to California recognized that the nation's economic future was heavily dependent on coal production. Coal's main rival as a source of energy was oil. In the 1840s, the oil industry barely existed. When engineers developed new ways of accessing oil in the 1850s and inventors figured out new uses for it, the industry exploded. By the 1870s, a byproduct of oil, called kerosene, had replaced whale oil as the nation's main fuel for lanterns, and oil refineries developed forms of gasoline that were used as fuel oils, solvents, and lubricants. In the 1880s and 1890s, the oil industry emerged as a major economic force in the United States. This emergence was due partly to steadily rising demand for oil and partly to the uniting of the oil industry in the hands of one brilliant and ruthless entrepreneur: John D. Rockefeller. Rockefeller had entered the oil business in the early 1860s as a minor investor. By the end of the 1880s, though, he had built his Standard Oil Company into a financial empire without equal in the United States. It was the dominant producer, refiner, and seller of oil across the country. By the close of the 19th century, it had 20,000 oil wells, 4,000 miles (6,437 km) of pipeline, 5,000 tank rail cars, and more than 100,000 employees. It was thought to be the most feared and admired business in the world.

Steel Works

America's switch to coal and oil was of enormous benefit to the nation's iron industry, which used a series of innovations to transform itself into a maker of steel in the 1860s and 1870s. Steelmaking was expensive and time-consuming, so the substance generally was reserved for only special products, such as prairie plows and fine-edged tools.

In the 1860s, though, the Bessemer steelmaking process was introduced in iron foundries in England and the United States. This technological advance was named after Sir Henry Bessemer of England, but an American ironmaster named William Kelly actually made the same breakthrough at roughly the same time. Both men discovered a method of creating steel by using air to remove excess carbon and other impurities in molten iron. Armed with this innovation, iron makers were able to process steel in far greater volumes than ever before.

Steel was a much stronger and more reliable product than iron, so when steel production became commercially viable, the impact was felt across the U.S. economy. Steel became the material of choice for railroad lines and the skyscrapers that rose in numerous cities. By 1880, annual American steel production reached 1.25 million tons (1.13 million metric tonnes). By 1900, this number was an incredible 10 million tons (9 million mt). During this time, the industry became one of the country's leading employers of Irish, German, Russian, Italian, Polish, and English immigrants.

Many of these immigrants went to work for Andrew Carnegie. The Carnegie Steel Company, which was led by Carnegie and his partner Henry Clay Frick, had been carefully constructed in the 1870s and 1880s so that it had a presence in every aspect of the steel industry. Carnegie's personal secretary, James Howard Bridge, recalled that by the early 1890s, the Carnegie steel empire

A color engraving reveals the inside of the Carnegie Steel Works in Pittsburgh, Pennsylvania, in 1886.

> *owned its own mines, dug its ore with machines of amazing power, loaded it into its own steamers, landed it at its own ports, transported it on its own railroads, distributed it among its many blast-furnaces, and smelted it with coke similarly brought from its own coal-mines and ovens, and with*

limestone brought from its own quarries. From the moments these crude stuffs were dug out of the earth until they flowed in a stream of liquid steel into the ladles, there was never a price, profit, or royalty paid to an outsider.[3]

By the end of the 19th century, Carnegie Steel not only was America's leading steelmaker but it also was producing more steel than the entire British steel industry.

Economic Synergy

Clearly, the Industrial Age was not about one industry. Instead, it was about many businesses, inventions, processes, and innovations working together to create a world of changes. The emergence of Carnegie Steel and the American steel industry could not have happened without coal's rise and availability as a foundry fuel. The steel industry also could not have risen to such great heights without the development of American railroads, with their demand for steel rails. The steel industry, in turn, had an immense influence on the real estate industry because it provided the raw material to construct factories, railroad depots, bridges, dams, harbors, and office buildings that American cities needed. Similarly, cattle ranches out west saw profits rise after the 1870s, when refrigerated railcars could deliver beef to faraway markets.

In fact, as historian John Steele Gordon noted, the necessities of the railroad industry drove an assortment of manufacturers:

Railroads required enormous quantities of industrial goods: locomotives, freight and passenger cars, rails, cross ties, spikes, and bridge members, to name just a few. At first, nearly all these had to be imported from England. But as the American demand for these commodities grew, more and more American entrepreneurs began to supply them, driving the Industrial Revolution in this country more than any other single force.[4]

Perhaps no industry benefited more from the railroads than the telegraph industry. American inventor Samuel F. B. Morse had unveiled his telegraph in 1837 and improved it in 1838. Beginning in

THEY MADE HISTORY: SAMUEL F. B. MORSE

Samuel Finley Breese Morse was born on April 27, 1791, in Charlestown, Massachusetts. The son of a minister, he attended Yale University and spent several years studying painting in England. Morse eventually established a thriving portrait studio in Boston, Massachusetts. In the early 1830s, he became fascinated with early experiments with electromagnetism, which some scientists theorized could be harnessed to send messages long distances over wire.

Morse teamed with Alfred Vail to build a telegraph prototype that could transmit electrical pulses of varying length—an alphabet of dots and dashes that came to be known as Morse code—over electrical wires to stations miles apart. Morse received a patent for his telegraph invention in 1837, and in 1843, he received a long-sought grant from the U.S. Congress to build a telegraph line between Washington, D.C., and Baltimore, Maryland. Months later, on May 24, 1844, he successfully transmitted a message between the Washington and Baltimore stations: "What hath God wrought!" Word of this triumph triggered a frenzy of telegraph network building up and down the East Coast.

During the second half of the 19th century, Morse's invention spread across the United States and changed American life forever. It also made the inventor a wealthy man. In his later years, Morse divided his time between charitable efforts, political activism, and his large family. He died in New York City on April 2, 1872.

In the mid-1800s, Samuel Morse's telegraph technology was the fastest way to communicate over a long distance. It quickly spread around the world.

the 1840s, telegraph wires were strung up across the United States, at first between eastern cities.

John Steele Gordon explained the telegraph's importance:

> *It is hard to imagine today . . . just how slowly news spread in the eighteenth century. The battles of Lexington and Concord, the opening events of the American Revolution, occurred on Wednesday, April 19, 1775. But news of the events reached New York only on Sunday, April 23, and Philadelphia on April 24 . . . And it was on May 28, fully five and a half weeks later, that the British cabinet in London learned, to its horror, that the long-smoldering crisis in America had flashed into open war.*[5]

The telegraph system changed that. Suddenly, people could communicate across hundreds or even thousands of miles nearly instantly. By 1854, there were about 23,000 miles (37,015 km) of telegraph wire. By the 1860s, they were following railroad lines out into the western frontier.

The telegraph needed the path that railroads were providing to the West. The railroad corridors saved the telegraph companies a lot of money. In turn, the railroads needed the telegraph to help organize the arrival and departure of trains. (This was especially important on single-track routes, on which trains traveling toward each other could collide.)

The telegraph and railroad's alliance was similar to others in the American business world. At times, these alliances helped forge enormous corporations that had great control over the marketplace. By the end of the 1800s, some of these corporate giants held so much power that the American public rebelled, demanding change.

How You See History

1. What people might have been against the idea of Manifest Destiny, and why?
2. Why do you think the robber barons were admired by some, although they sometimes employed unscrupulous tactics?
3. Name some ways that the telegraph might have helped people and industries in the 1800s.

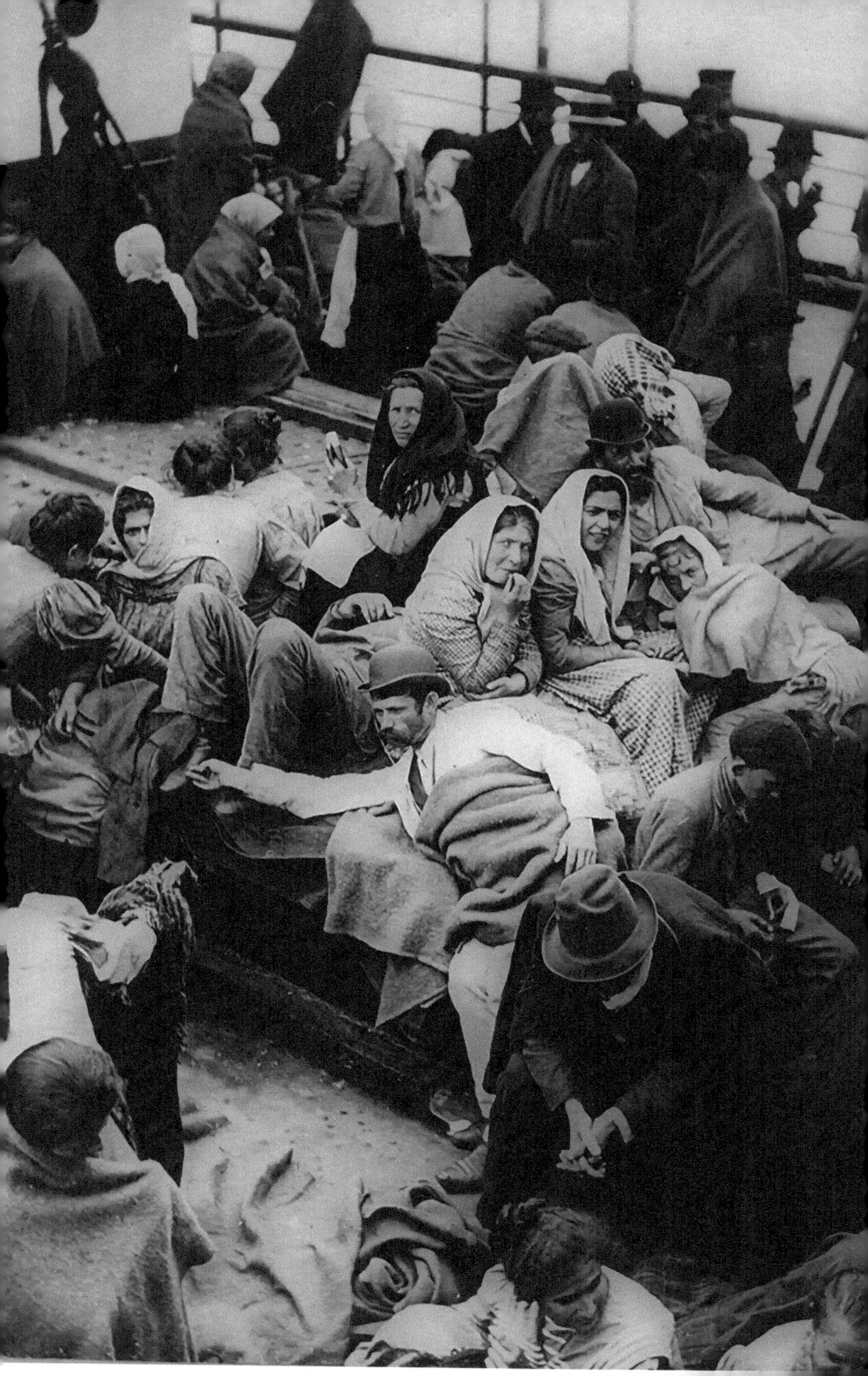

CHAPTER FOUR

TRANSFORMED BY INDUSTRY

Undoubtedly, the Industrial Revolution improved many people's lives in countless ways. The telegraph allowed people to share news. The railroad brought them to their loved ones in less time. New inventions made homes more comfortable, and a growing number of people found themselves capable of buying more goods. However, the Industrial Age did not bring wealth and happiness to everyone. The expanding nation meant the end of traditions and the loss of ancestral lands to Native Americans in the West. Americans settling in newly opened regions battled many challenging obstacles. In urban areas, only a select few became rich. Many workers suffered because of poor wages and difficult working conditions. In fact, some factories were downright dangerous. As the 19th century wore on, tensions rose between laborers and employers as laborers demanded better treatment.

The United States was changing in other ways too. Women's roles were evolving, whether they were out in the workforce or at home. More women began asking for equal rights, specifically the right to vote. Children made a transition out of homes, mines, and factories and into classrooms as education became a priority at the end of the 19th century. Also in transition was the very makeup of the American people. Increasing numbers of immigrants and their movements within

The journey to find work and build a life in America was not an easy one. You can see the uncomfortable, crowded conditions in this photograph taken on a ship approaching New York City.

the country changed the face of the nation. The Industrial Revolution roared on, largely thanks to them.

From Europe to the United States

One key to America's rapid industrialization and settlement of the West was the massive, sustained immigration of Europeans during the 19th century. This wave of immigration stemmed in part from problems in Europe, where political turmoil, lack of economic opportunity, and crop failures afflicted many regions. European immigrants made the long and difficult journey across the Atlantic Ocean with optimism and hope. They knew that factory jobs and inexpensive land for farming awaited them in America. To these struggling men and women, the United States represented a fresh start.

Between 1850 and 1860, about 2.5 million immigrants arrived in the United States. Most settled in Northern cities, but many went to the West. As the 19th century went on, the flood of immigrants did not slow. Instead, the source of European immigration merely shifted from Germany, England, and other western European nations to Italy, Poland, and other parts of eastern Europe.

Whatever their country of origin, these European immigrants—as well as smaller numbers of immigrants from other places, including Mexico, China, and the West Indies—became essential to America's stunning economic growth. Many filled factories, steel mills, shipyards, coal mines, and oil fields, where they operated great industrial machines that rattled and roared around the clock.

Some immigrants and their families lived hundreds of miles from the nearest city, but they contributed to the Industrial Age as well. After all, it was their labor that provided the food, coal, iron ore, and other resources that kept the cities humming. Many staked their futures on the Great Lakes region or the territories of the Great Plains, where they established farms or joined logging and mining companies. The immigrants who settled in rural areas of the central United States and the Great Plains faced many trials. Some obstacles, such as weather-related crop failures and high railroad freight charges, were challenges throughout the rural regions. Others were unique to certain areas. In various parts of the West, for example, settlers, miners, and ranchers entered

PAST MEETS PRESENT: IMMIGRATION ISSUES

Thousands of Chinese people came to California in the mid-1800s looking for economic opportunities that were not available in their homeland. Some worked in mines. Many were crucial in the building of the transcontinental railroad, accomplishing dangerous tasks that others would not do, such as handling blasting materials. Though they were a valuable part of the American workforce, the Chinese were often treated poorly, forced to accept lower wages and to work longer hours. Still, many Americans believed the Chinese were "stealing" jobs from others and sought to stop more Chinese from coming to America. In 1882, they got their wish. A law called the Chinese Exclusion Act halted immigration from China for at least 10 years. Those Chinese who did live in America were forced to carry identification. This was the first legislation of its kind, limiting the rights of immigrants and stopping a specific group of people from coming to America. However, it would not be the last. Other laws would be passed to limit immigrants from certain countries until such practices ended in 1965.

Immigration continues to be a hot-button issue. Events such as the terrorist attacks of September 11, 2001, have made some Americans distrustful of certain groups of legal immigrants. Some Americans worry, too, that immigrants, who often do low-paying jobs, are taking opportunities from natural-born citizens. There is little consensus about how to solve the disagreements surrounding these issues.

into violent conflict with Native Americans desperate to stop the white invaders from taking their lands and destroying their ways of life.

Nonetheless, many immigrant families who settled in U.S. cities would have gladly changed places with their rural counterparts. Working-class people in New York, Chicago, and other major cities lived in troubled surroundings. American cities grew so quickly that

HISTORY HAPPENED HERE: WOUNDED KNEE MONUMENT

Wounded Knee Monument in South Dakota marks the site of a tragedy for the Oglala Sioux people. In the late 1800s, the Oglala were forced onto a reservation. They had experienced decades of white settlers, miners, and government officials pushing them off their historic lands. The Sioux had been nomadic people, following large herds of bison that they relied on for most of their food. However, settlers began hunting bison, too, killing them until there were few left for the needs of Native Americans. A settled life on a reservation meant that the Oglala Sioux's traditional life was over. They began to starve.

The despondent Oglala began to follow the teachings of a Native American religious leader named Wovoka. He promised that performing the ceremony called the Ghost Dance would drive the white people away. The U.S. government decided this movement needed to be stopped. On December 15, 1890, reservation police killed Chief Sitting Bull while trying to arrest him at Standing Rock Reservation. Hundreds of Sioux then fled their homes and followed Chief Big Foot, who headed toward the Pine Ridge Reservation. The Sioux were not allowed to leave their own reservation, so U.S. soldiers pursued them. The Native Americans surrendered on December 28. The next day, near Wounded Knee Creek, the U.S. troops began taking the Native Americans' weapons away. Someone fired a shot, killing a soldier. More shots began to ring out. By the end, more than 140 Native Americans were killed, including 16 children.

The Wounded Knee Monument marks the site of a mass grave for the Native Americans who died during what some called a battle and others called a massacre.

governments were overwhelmed. Poverty, disease, and crime filled the streets of many crowded urban neighborhoods. Millions of young children were forced by economic circumstances to work next to their parents in factories and mills.

Many immigrants tried to shield themselves from problems by gathering in ethnic enclaves. In these neighborhoods, people could take comfort in their native languages and customs. These settlement patterns, though, cultivated mistrust and prejudice between isolated ethnic groups who often competed for jobs and housing.

Fighting for Change

As industrialization swept across America, immigrant and native-born workers alike expressed anger and frustration with their corporate employers. Most industries expected long hours of hard work from their unskilled and semiskilled workers. Extremely long workweeks—60 or 70 hours—were common, and many jobs took a significant physical toll. Workers were almost always paid poorly, and they often endured hazardous working conditions. In fact, employers had no legal responsibility for injuries or deaths suffered in their factories, and few owners felt any moral obligation to keep their employees safe. In the early 20th century, more than 23,000 industrial workers were killed annually, and another 1 million suffered injury. "By present standards the age of America's first Industrial Revolution must be regarded as callous in its relative indifference to the welfare and safety of workers," described historian Stuart Bruchey. "The unemployed worker was cast adrift. As a rule, there was no such thing as public relief, and private charity was either insufficient or offered only on demeaning terms. The risks of injury or death on the job were grievously high."[1]

American workers tried to change working conditions by joining together in labor unions. These unions bargained with employers on behalf of their members on a range of issues. They sought better wages and benefits, shorter work hours, more flexible work rules, and safer working conditions. In the post–Civil War era, some unions of skilled craftsmen did manage to negotiate significant wage and workplace improvements for their members. However, unskilled and semiskilled workers did not have the same bargaining power. Their efforts to

THEY MADE HISTORY: UPTON SINCLAIR

The famous American journalist Upton Sinclair was born September 20, 1878, in Baltimore, Maryland. He set out to make a career for himself as a writer and investigative reporter at an early age. Sinclair did not achieve fame, though, until he published *The Jungle* in 1906. This novel painted such a grim—and accurate—picture of the horrible conditions in the U.S. meatpacking industry that the American public demanded reforms. Congress and President Theodore Roosevelt responded by passing the Pure Food and Drug Act and the Meat Inspection Act in 1906.

The uproar over *The Jungle* established Sinclair as the most prominent of America's muckrakers—a term that was initially mockingly applied to a group of journalists who used their writing to expose political corruption, social problems, and corporate trickery. As the years passed, Sinclair wrote dozens of novels, essays, and investigative reports. Many of these works reflected the author's commitment to social justice and his strong belief in socialism.

Upton Sinclair had hoped to arouse people's sympathies for workers in his book *The Jungle*. He also memorably provided graphic descriptions of the production of meat in the book.

In the 1920s, Sinclair's political activism led him to make two unsuccessful bids for Congress. In 1934, he won the Democratic nomination for California's governorship with a platform he called EPIC (End Poverty in California), but he was defeated by Republican nominee Frank Merriam in the general election. Sinclair returned to writing, and in 1943, he received the Pulitzer Prize for his novel *Dragon's Teeth*. Sinclair died November 25, 1968.

improve their circumstances and better provide for their families were typically crushed by corporate owners determined to maximize their profits. Sometimes, mining, railroad, and manufacturing companies with political influence called in local police or even National Guard troops to break strikes and harass union leaders. The ruthless strategies of America's corporate giants made it hard for unions to make significant gains, and union membership remained low—further hurting their bargaining power.

Despite disappointments, activists such as Samuel Gompers of the American Federation of Labor (AFL), John Mitchell of the United Mine Workers of America (UMWA), labor leader Mary Harris "Mother" Jones, populist politician William Jennings Bryan, and Socialist Eugene Debs continued to fight for workers' rights in the late 1800s and early 1900s. Their calls for economic and social justice were echoed by journalists such as Upton Sinclair, Ida Tarbell, and Jacob Riis. The stories published by these investigative reporters detailed crushing poverty in slums, brutal working conditions in factories, and ways in which big business manipulated the nation's political, judicial, and economic systems.

Regulating Business

By the dawn of the 20th century, public calls for business and social reform were impossible to ignore. Many middle-class people had joined working-class critics in concluding that the wealthy industrialists who directed the country's huge corporations and trusts were more concerned with economic and political power than the well-being of their fellow citizens. These Americans welcomed the economic growth and excitement that industrialization had brought, but they worried that big business bore a heavy responsibility for the poverty and political corruption that troubled the nation. "The rise of large-scale corporations was unsettling, even frightening," wrote scholar Michael McGerr. He added:

> *United States Steel, Standard Oil, and the rest were certainly remarkable creations . . . they provided a host of new goods and services, often at lower costs ... [But] they wielded disturbing economic power: more than one industry had become an oligopoly, basically controlled by a handful of large firms. The corporations could hurt*

consumers by raising the price of goods; they could hurt farmers and businessmen by raising railroad rates and hiking the cost of raw materials; they could hurt workers by cutting wages and demanding more productivity; they could hurt competitors by slashing the price of finished products and raising the price of raw materials; they could hurt towns, cities, whole regions of the country by manipulating freight charges and putting railroads and factories in one locale or another.[2]

This unhappiness with the direction of American society became so profound that political leaders finally responded. They passed laws designed to diminish the power of the corporate giants and address social problems created by industrialization. "The captains of industry who have driven the railway systems across this continent, who have built up our commerce, who have developed our manufactures, have on the whole done great good to our people," President Theodore Roosevelt admitted in 1901. "Yet it is also true that there are real and grave evils [in corporate America] … a resolute and practical effort must be made to correct these evils."[3]

From the 1890s through 1920, numerous laws were passed to lessen the influence of big business and increase the rights of workers. Some of these laws were ineffective, but others did reduce exploitation of workers, help the elderly, decrease the use of child labor, and eliminate business monopolies in certain industries. All of this legislation ushered in a new chapter in American history: From this point forward, the U.S. government would take a much more active role in regulating business activity and addressing social problems.

Women in the Industrialized World

The Industrial Revolution triggered major changes in the lives of women. Prior to industrialization, men and women carried out the work necessary to thrive in America's farm-oriented economy. Most duties were divided based on gender. Men had greater responsibility for fieldwork, while women spent more of their time tending to housework and raising children. Nonetheless, husbands and wives generally worked as a team to make their farms successful, and they often spent time with each other over the course of a day.

As the Industrial Revolution swept across the United States, this changed. Large numbers of families left rural America for the fast-growing cities. Once they settled in cities, men took factory jobs, and women were left to take care of the children and numerous household chores associated with 19th-century life. Some young women entered the industrial world as well—most visibly in the New England textile mills—but they generally were segregated from male workers, and they often left these jobs once they married and started families.

By the mid-19th century, industrialization had expanded the need for clerks, managers, engineers, and skilled craftsmen, all of whom became members of the nation's ever-growing middle class. Men almost always filled these positions, leaving their wives with more leisure time, yet women's opportunities for personal growth were, in some ways, more limited than ever before. The men who dominated industrialized society came to view the home as a relaxing break from the factory floors and corporate offices in which they worked. They wanted their wives and daughters to devote their energies and talents to the home and leave the messy arenas of business and politics to men. In this culture, the most highly prized women were those who displayed good manners, high morals, and quiet obedience to husbands and fathers.

Some women, though, openly rebelled at these restrictions. They wanted to end their exclusion from the new business world that industrialization had created. They also wanted increased access to higher education and greater freedom to make their own life choices and their own judgments about "moral" and "appropriate" behavior. Finally, they wanted more of a voice in politics. They knew if they had suffrage—the right to vote—they could have more control over issues that were important to them.

Some women worked in factories to earn their own money and to establish their independence. Others had no choice; they needed the money. Either way, it was not easy labor.

FROM THE SOURCE: SUSAN B. ANTHONY'S SPEECH

Susan B. Anthony, one of the most famous proponents for women's rights in the 19th century, was arrested in 1872 for voting in the U.S. presidential election. At the time, women could not legally vote. After her arrest, she gave a speech in which she said:

> *I stand before you tonight under indictment for the alleged crime of having voted at the last presidential election, without having a lawful right to vote . . . The preamble of the Federal Constitution says: "We, the people of the United States, in order to form a more perfect union, establish justice, insure domestic tranquillity, provide for the common defense, promote the general welfare, and secure the blessings of liberty to ourselves and our posterity, do ordain and establish this Constitution for the United States of America." It was we, the people; not we, the white male citizens . . . it is a downright mockery to talk to women of their enjoyment*

All of these factors contributed to campaigns for suffrage and women's rights in the second half of the 19th century. The birth of the women's rights movement in America is often traced to an 1848 convention at Seneca Falls, New York, that was organized by Elizabeth Cady Stanton and Lucretia Mott. At first, people ridiculed the movement or simply ignored it. Time and time again, however, activists successfully framed the issue of suffrage as one of basic justice.

Public support for suffrage and women's rights strengthened throughout the last decades of the 19th century. The battle continued into the early 20th century under a new generation of leaders, such as Alice Paul and Carrie Chapman Catt. In 1920, the right to vote was finally extended to American women when the 19th Amendment became part of the U.S. Constitution.

The Advent of Public Education

The Industrial Revolution had a significant impact on the American education system. Prior to the 1830s, a national public school *of the blessings of liberty while they are denied the use of the only means of securing them provided by this democratic-republican government—the ballot . . . The only question left to be settled now is: Are women persons? And I hardly believe any of our opponents will have the hardihood to say they are not. Being persons, then, women are citizens; and no state has a right to make any law, or to enforce any old law, that shall abridge their privileges or immunities.*[1]

Susan B. Anthony was a tireless champion for women's rights. She died March 13, 1906. It was another 14 years before American women received suffrage at last.

1. Susan B. Anthony, "On Women's Right to Vote," Digital History, www.digitalhistory.uh.edu/disp_textbook.cfm?smtid=3&psid=3604 (accessed October 4, 2020).

system did not exist in the United States. Formal schooling was not even available in some parts of the country, and children of wealthy families received far greater levels of instruction (often from private tutors) than did children from poor, working-class, or even middle-class backgrounds.

In the 1830s and 1840s, New England reformers began calling for the establishment of free public schools across the country. Despite the fact that these schools would be paid for through higher taxes, major manufacturing companies were among the most enthusiastic supporters. Their influence with lawmakers made passage of laws supporting public schools more likely.

In 1852, Massachusetts passed the nation's first mandatory school attendance laws. Many other states quickly followed, although it was not until 1918 that all states had such laws in place. During the second half of the 19th century, state legislatures moved to provide funding for public schools for all American children. By the end of the 1800s, free elementary public school systems were in place in every state. In 1925,

Many young Americans in the 1800s went to a school like this, in which children of many ages shared one classroom.

though, Catholic opposition to compulsory public schooling led to a U.S. Supreme Court ruling that permitted parents to enroll children in private schools. This mix of public and private elementary and high schools remains in place today.

Everyday Life

As much as life in the workplace changed in the United States in the 1800s, so did life in the community and at home. The Industrial Revolution was the source of this transformation as well.

The very look of cities was altered as streets were lit at night by gaslights. Steel made it possible for tall buildings, soon to be called skyscrapers, to be constructed. Public transit systems began to arise with streetcars taking people to their destinations. Even something as simple and fundamental as the water supply was transformed. From 1850 to 1900, the number of public water systems grew from 83 to 3,000. A clean and ready water supply was essential in both fighting diseases carried by polluted water, such as cholera, and fighting fires that inevitably arose in crowded cities.

Advances in transportation, too, opened new worlds of opportunity, recreation, and adventure for Americans. Railroads were just one transportation option of the age. Huge ocean liners clad in steel and propelled by improved engines ferried people across the ocean at new speeds. Before the early 1800s, historian John Steele Gordon observed:

> *People seldom ventured more than fifty miles from where they had been born, or, if they did, never saw their birthplace again. Now, in less than a lifetime, it had become possible to travel a hundred miles*

in a day, receive instant word from someone a thousand miles away, and read of events that were taking place, right then, halfway around the world. It was possible to have hot water run out of a tap, be warm on the coldest night, read a book at night without eyestrain.[4]

The industrialization of businesses also led to consumerism in American society. Though many people still could not afford to partake in purchasing nonessential goods, a growing middle class found itself with disposable income to buy more goods, many of which were less expensive because they were mass-produced rather than made by hand. Among the wide array of products available were processed foods, decorative furniture, household cleaning products, toys and games, and ready-made clothing, things people once made for themselves. With the rise of consumer goods came the rise of large stores that sold them. Department stores were introduced around the turn of the 20th century, some of which still survive today, such as Macy's.

The same people who could afford more consumer goods also found themselves with more leisure time. They turned to recreational activities such as bicycling and fishing as well as live entertainment such as musicals, stage shows, and circuses. Spectator sports, too, became popular. Football, basketball, horse racing, wrestling, and boxing caught people's interest. In fact, notable athletes of the era, such as boxer John L. Sullivan, were among the most famous figures across the nation. As the United States entered a new century, it may have been hard for some to believe that life could change more than it already had. In fact, though, new inventions were poised to connect people as never before.

How You See History

1. How did white settlers and the U.S. government change the Native American way of life?
2. Why do you think major industries supported the idea of free public school education?
3. What parts of the shifting social life of the late 1800s do you recognize in today's American culture?

CHAPTER FIVE

NEW DEVELOPMENTS IN THE 1900S

While the most transformative elements of the Industrial Age hit their peak in the 19th century, innovations and inventions continued to appear in the early 20th century. They could not have come about without the advances of the century before.

Among the most celebrated and enduring inventions that established themselves in the early 1900s were the telephone, radio, television, and automobile. American innovators such as Alexander Graham Bell and Henry Ford made these concepts into reality in the United States—and made products that many Americans could own and use. Meanwhile, the Wright brothers achieved a feat that inventors had chased for centuries when they took flight in an airplane in 1903. Like with the railroad in the previous century, transportation would be forever changed by this achievement. American businesses used these inventions and others to propel the United States into economic dominance in the world.

Long-Distance Calls

An invention that changed business and culture in the 20th century, the telephone, had actually been introduced in the 1870s. However, Alexander Graham Bell's device did not replace the telegraph as the nation's leading communication tool until the early 1900s.

In the early days of the telephone, an operator connected a call between two people through a switchboard. Many switchboard operators were women.

In its earliest decades, the telephone industry was dominated by the Bell Telephone Company and its long-distance service company, American Telephone & Telegraph (AT&T). This near-monopoly was brief, though. Bell remained the industry's giant, but by 1900, smaller companies were supplying service to telephone owners across the country too. The independent companies could not compete with Bell in the big cities, but they prospered in more rural areas of the country.

These smaller firms were able to survive because of steadily rising demand for the telephone. Indeed, Bell's invention swept across the country with amazing speed. By 1880, 50,000 telephones were in use in the United States. By 1900, that number was 1.35 million. By 1930, telephone ownership had skyrocketed to more than 20 million. The benefits of the telephone were clear to nearly everyone. It aided business enterprises and government agencies, and it enabled people to talk to friends and family who lived far away. The telephone was particularly treasured in rural communities because it helped ward off feelings of isolation and loneliness that haunted many farming families.

During the 1920s and 1930s, the telephone industry continued to grow, defying the economic downturn of the Great Depression. AT&T (which had become the parent company to Bell in 1899) reestablished its monopoly over the industry, and it became more advanced and widespread with every passing year. By 1940, the company had established phone service to millions of American homes and businesses and opened international service. "From World War I to 1940," wrote historian Claude Fischer, "competition almost ceased as the companies divided the telephone business among themselves under the hegemony [control] of AT&T and the supervision of federal and state regulators. The telephone system remained essentially the same as it was on the eve of World War II until the court-ordered dismemberment [break up] of AT&T forty-four years later."[1]

Broadcast Radio

Wireless broadcast radio was another major milestone of the Industrial Age. This breakthrough in communication technology gave American business a new avenue through which it could advertise products and services. It also began a new era of popular entertainment and became a centerpiece of family life throughout the first half of the 20th century.

Late-19th-century inventors and scientists, such as Guglielmo Marconi and Nikola Tesla, were among the first to experiment with harnessing radio waves for long-distance communication. During the 1900s and 1910s, European and American engineers and entrepreneurs built on their work, refining the technology and experimenting with ways to harness radio's possibilities for profit. It was not until the early 1920s that commercial radio broadcasting became a reality. In 1920, KDKA, a station based in Pittsburgh, became the first government-licensed commercial radio broadcasting station in the United States. Over the next few years, hundreds more stations scrambled to get recognized and receive their licenses.

The 1920s were years of general economic prosperity and optimism in the United States, and many Americans came to view radio—along with the automobile—as one of the strongest symbols of this miraculous new age. American families loved the fact that they could now hear live musical performances, sporting events, comedy shows, news headlines, and all sorts of other entertainment in their living rooms with the turn of a dial, and they rushed to purchase radio sets and equipment from local stores. In 1925, reports estimated that 5 million U.S. homes, or nearly 20 percent, had radio sets. As historians Robert Hilliard and Michael Keith have noted, the new technology quickly replaced newspapers as the country's preferred source of news and entertainment:

> *The prosperity and brashness of the Roaring Twenties, including the increasing domination of big business over the economy, gave importance to radio's live, national advertising potential . . . By and large it was a time of affluence [wealth] and material possessions, the growth of a new economic middle class, new*

Broadcaster Frank Mullen speaks into the microphone at station KDKA in 1922.

opportunities through mass production for unskilled and skilled workers, and a national devil-may-care euphoria. Radio fit perfectly into this heady postwar world, sometimes informing, sometimes educating, sometimes assuaging, and mostly entertaining.[2]

The leading radio broadcasters of this era were the Columbia Broadcasting System (CBS) and the National Broadcasting Company (NBC), both of which developed impressive national networks of local radio stations. These networks became even more valuable after passage of the Radio Act of 1927. This act created the Federal Radio Commission (FRC) to oversee and regulate aspects of broadcasting. For NBC, CBS, and other industry participants, however, the most important duty of the FRC was to assign specific radio frequencies to individual stations. This change brought much-needed order to the airwaves. The number of radio stations had grown so quickly that the entire industry had been in danger of smothering itself in a huge storm of competing radio signals.

As it turned out, broadcast radio's position as America's leading source of news and entertainment would be short-lived. Radio continues to exist as a popular source of music, entertainment, and news, and millions still listen to public, commercial, or satellite radio daily. In the 1950s, however, a new communications medium called television became popular, and American business and society were changed forever.

Introducing Television Technology

The earliest television technology grew out of the work of numerous inventors, scientists, and engineers at the beginning of the 20th century, but the first working electronic television systems did not appear until the 1920s. At that time, the CBS and NBC radio networks took the lead in pursuing commercial applications for this dawning technology. Several executives and inventors provided important contributions to television technology during this time, including Philo Farnsworth and Vladimir Zworykin.

Perhaps no one was as important to the industry's development as David Sarnoff, who headed the Radio Corporation of America (RCA)—the parent company of NBC. Sarnoff was convinced that television was the world's next great leap in communication, and he worked

David Sarnoff, president of RCA and head of NBC, immigrated to the United States from Russia as a young boy.

tirelessly to see his vision become a reality.

In the 1930s, some companies, including NBC and CBS, began experimenting with commercial television broadcasts. These early efforts were largely ignored. The Great Depression dampened public interest in the new technology, and World War II brought almost all television manufacturing and broadcasting activity to a halt. After the war, American households found themselves riding a wave of major economic prosperity. Armed with well-paying jobs—and eager to put memories of the Depression and war behind them—families rushed to buy televisions. Television ownership, which was less than 20 percent of American homes in 1950, rose to nearly 90 percent by 1960. The introduction of color television sets gave another big boost to television's popularity, and by the early 1970s, a large portion of the nation's sets were color.

Today, decades after it first burst onto the cultural scene, television remains an influential presence in the lives of nearly all Americans. It is a major source of information and entertainment and has long ranked as a leading medium for marketing products and services to consumers.

Motoring into the 20th Century

The third major innovation that transformed American business and society in the early 20th century was the automobile. This industry came out of Detroit, Michigan, in the opening years of the century. By the 1910s, it was clear that this invention was becoming an important part of American life. From 1900 to 1910 alone, the total number of cars produced in the United States rose dramatically—from 4,000 to 187,000.

Automobiles were created during this period by hundreds of small companies. The single most influential automobile in America, though,

PAST MEETS PRESENT: TELEVISION TODAY

From the 1950s through the 1970s, nearly all television programming came from three networks of allied local stations. These networks—CBS, NBC, and ABC—began as radio networks. CBS was formed in 1927 through the merger of United Independent Broadcasters, which was a radio broadcasting company, and the Columbia Phonograph Company. NBC had been launched one year earlier by RCA, which was one of the nation's largest radio manufacturers. NBC grew so large that it divided itself into two radio networks, called Red and Blue. In 1943, concerns about NBC's growing monopoly led the U.S. government to force NBC to sell off its Blue network. This network became the basis for the American Broadcasting Company (ABC).

While public television stations and a small number of independent stations operated as well, none had the financial resources to compete with the big networks. The Big Three divided up virtually all American viewers until the 1970s, when improved technology enabled new cable television stations to emerge on the scene. When cable subscription services and then satellite networks became popular, some predicted the demise of broadcast television. Cable took in revenue from advertising and its subscribers, while the networks relied on advertising only. Later, when subscription-based streaming services such as Netflix, Apple TV, and Amazon Prime arrived, many Americans began "cutting the cord" of their cable service. Even the CBS and NBC networks began their own subscription services in addition to their traditional networks. Many wonder if the abundance of subscription services will force another change in the television industry in the future.

was the Model T, which was introduced by Henry Ford in 1908. Reliable and affordable, the Model T ushered in the Age of the Automobile. By 1920, Ford's vehicles accounted for more than 60 percent of the motor vehicles in the country. This was possible because of Ford's

Ford employees are pictured working on an assembly line in a factory in Highland Park, Michigan, in 1914.

assembly line system of production. In this relatively new form of organizing employees, each worker was responsible for just one component of the car, and when they finished their section, the product was sent on to the next person in the assembly line. His stunning success made Ford one of the most admired individuals in the history of American business.

The rapid spread of the automobile was greatly aided by the introduction of credit purchasing plans. Throughout most of American history, if someone wanted something, they most likely paid for it with cash—in full. Purchasing something on credit was almost the exact opposite of this. If someone wanted to buy a car, for example, they would make a down payment with their dealer (typically 10 or 20 percent of the price) and promise to pay off the rest over time. Credit plans were important to the growth of the automobile industry since the purchase of an automobile—from the cheapest to the most luxurious—carried a considerable price tag that few American families could pay in cash.

By the end of the 1920s, motor vehicles had spread to all corners of the United States. By 1929, there were approximately 27 million vehicles on American roads. This growth not only reflected enthusiasm for the freedom these cars provided but also the rising importance of car and truck transportation to other industries.

The Automobile's Effects

By the end of the 1920s, carmakers were consuming a significant percentage of the nation's wood, iron, steel, and aluminum. The industry also prompted new waves of road and highway construction, commercial development, and residential housing construction across the country. Finally, automobile owners needed gasoline to run their machines, so they became a leading source of income for oil producers.

The Great Depression of the 1930s took a heavy toll on automakers. However, the demand for planes, tanks, clothing, food, and other goods

THEY MADE HISTORY: HENRY FORD

Famed automaker Henry Ford was born in Michigan in 1863. He studied and worked to be an engineer, and in the early 1890s, he took a job with Thomas Edison's Detroit Illuminating Company. Ford began experimenting with automobile designs, and by the end of the century, he had built several working prototypes. These successes attracted the attention of investors, and in 1903, he launched the Ford Motor Company.

In 1908, Ford unveiled a new automobile, the Model T, which ranks as the most famous and influential automobile in the history of the industry. Ford was able to sell the reliable Model T at a price that attracted middle-class buyers because his introduction of the assembly line kept production costs low. Ford's assembly line was quickly adopted by other industries, and it remains a feature of modern industrial manufacturing.

Ford built an automotive empire during the 1910s and 1920s, and his 1914 decision to pay his workers a high wage further boosted his reputation as one of America's finest citizens. He was a generous donor who established hospitals and charitable foundations that exist well into the 21st century. As time passed, his reputation as a hero was tarnished by his prejudicial views against Jewish people, his controlling attitude toward his workforce, and his ruthless attempts to stifle labor unions. In 1945, Ford turned over the reins of the company to his grandson, Henry Ford II, and retired. He died at his Dearborn, Michigan, estate in 1947.

during World War II got factories roaring again. When the United States emerged from the war in 1945, it entered a period of economic prosperity that lasted through the 1950s. Ford Motor Company, General Motors, and the Chrysler Corporation—the so-called Big Three of U.S. automakers—reaped the benefits of the rising economy. In the decade after World War II, the number of passenger cars on American roads shot up to more than 50 million. The profits of oil companies jumped as well, as gasoline consumption soared.

The Ford Model T, shown here, was sold from 1908 to 1927. It was the earliest affordable car. Between 1913 and 1927, factories produced more than 15 million Model Ts, thanks to the assembly line.

The midcentury growth of America's oil companies provided a clear example of the importance of the auto industry to the nation's economic health. When automakers suffered declines in sales, the ripples were felt in other industries; when automakers thrived, the entire economy benefited. "If any industry represented America's industrial might in the 20th century, surely it was auto makers," a report in *Bloomberg Businessweek* asserted. "The handful of companies clustered around Detroit produced the assembly line in 1913, tanks and aircraft engines during World War II, and thousands of high-paying factory jobs when peace came. The industry became the backbone of the U.S. economy and its companies America's bellwethers [economic indicators]. As cars went, so went the nation."[3]

A New Industry Takes Flight

The last chapter in the Industrial Revolution's impact on transportation was written by the inventors and entrepreneurs who made air travel a reality. For centuries, people across the globe had dreamed of finding a way to take flight, but it was not until December 17, 1903, that this dream came true. On that day, brothers Orville and Wilbur Wright's motor-powered glider became airborne for a 12-second flight covering 120 feet (36.6 m) near Kitty Hawk, North Carolina.

Surprisingly, this did not attract a great deal of public attention when it occurred. Over the next few years, the Wright brothers and American and European inventors made a flurry of technological advances, but government and industry remained disinterested until World War I. At that time, European aircraft came to play such an important role in the conflict that U.S. officials and investors finally took a serious look at the airplane. During and after the war, America began to invest much more heavily in the industry. The U.S. Post Office introduced airmail service between Washington, D.C., and New York in 1918, and the military began acquiring airplanes in increasing numbers. This market gave a much-needed boost to early American aircraft makers.

The commercial potential of airplanes, meanwhile, became evident in May 1927, when American aviator Charles Lindbergh completed a nonstop flight from New York to Paris, France, over the course of two days. This feat made Lindbergh an international hero and convinced investors and ordinary Americans that long-distance flight could one day be a safe way to travel. It also gave momentum to governmental efforts to implement rules and regulations for the fast-growing industry. By the end of the 1920s, airplanes and pilots were subject to a number of licensing and operating regulations. In addition, the U.S. government passed laws that enabled private carriers to deliver mail. This became an important source of income for America's first generation of air carriers.

In the 1930s, U.S. and European aircraft continued to get bigger, stronger, and faster. Advances in engine and propeller design, landing gear, navigation instruments, and wing design made airplanes more efficient. This proved essential during World War II, when American air power helped the Allies defeat the Axis Powers. By the time the war ended in 1945, jet-powered engines were ready for use not only in military aircraft but also for business and travel.

During the 1950s and 1960s, advances in aeronautics came so quickly that technological marvels seemed to appear with each passing month. Supersonic flights, guided missiles, space satellites, and manned rockets designed for space exploration all burst out of the world of science fiction to become realities. Much of the investment and research that made these marvels possible came from the ongoing Cold War, a four-decade-long economic and military rivalry between the United States and the Soviet Union that began immediately after World War II. During this era, commercial air travel grew by leaps and bounds. By the mid-1970s, thousands of airports across America offered hundreds of thousands of flights to and from major eastern cities, rural western towns, and everywhere in between.

Buying Power

In the early 20th century, U.S. consumerism meant more than just individual Americans indulging in their spending whims. The collective

HISTORY HAPPENED HERE: WRIGHT BROTHERS NATIONAL MEMORIAL

The Wright brothers' success was a product of years of research and experimentation. In fact, though they lived in Ohio, they traveled to outside the town of Kitty Hawk, North Carolina, for three years before their first flight. There, they performed glider experiments in the hope of learning how to create a machine that could fly. They traveled all the way to North Carolina's Outer Banks, a chain of islands in eastern North Carolina, because it had the right amount of sand, wind, and remoteness to do their experiments safely and secretly.

Today, the Wright Brothers National Memorial in the town of Kill Devil Hills, North Carolina, encompasses the spot where Wilbur and Orville made their first flights in 1903. A monument stands on Kill Devil Hill, the sand dune off which Wilbur and Orville did many gliding experiments from 1900 to 1902. Visitors can also examine a replica of the 1903 flyer.

In this illustration of the famous flight, Wilbur watches as his brother Orville pilots their Wright Flyer plane. Later that day, Wilbur would pilot the plane in the air for 59 seconds.

force of Americans' increasing expenditures helped pull the country out of the Great Depression. Spending money became a patriotic duty in the 1950s, and the massive consumer economy that developed in the 1950s and 1960s introduced new elements of modern consumerism, such as the shopping mall, which made it convenient to spend money in many stores located close together. The credit card, first introduced in the 1950s, made it possible to spend money that the buyer may not

FROM THE SOURCE: ORVILLE WRIGHT'S DIARY ENTRY ABOUT THE FIRST FLIGHT

From 1900 to 1903, Orville and Wilbur Wright worked on kite and glider designs. On December 17, 1903, their efforts paid off in North Carolina. That day, Orville wrote in his diary:

I got on the machine at 10:35 for the first trial . . . On slipping the rope the machine started off increasing in speed to probably 7 or 8 miles . . . Mr. Daniels took a picture just as it left the tracks. I found the control of the front rudder quite difficult . . . As a result the machine would rise suddenly to about 10 ft. and then as suddenly, on turning the rudder, dart for the ground. A sudden dart when out about 100 feet from the end of the tracks ended the flight. Time about 12 seconds (not known exactly as watch was not promptly stopped.) . . .

At just 12 o'clock Will started on the fourth and last trip. The machine started off with its ups and downs as it had before, but by the time he had gone over three or four hundred feet he had it under much better control, and was traveling on a fairly even course. It proceeded in this manner till it reached a small hummock out about 800 feet from the starting ways, when it began its pitching again and suddenly darted into the ground. The front rudder frame was badly broken up, but the main frame suffered none at all. The distance over the ground was 852 feet in 59 seconds.[1]

1. Orville Wright, "First Flight," Smithsonian Education, www.smithsonianeducation.org/educators/lesson_plans/wright/first_flight.html (accessed October 7, 2020).

have on hand. Thus, there was no need to save money to buy a product in the future. Instead, it could be bought immediately and the amount would be paid back to the credit card company over time with interest owed. America became a nation of shoppers.

The surging economic power of the United States became obvious to everyone, and its importance to other countries became evident too. Business magazine *Fortune* declared in 1953:

> *All history can show no more portentous [significant] economic phenomenon than today's American market. It is colossal, soaking up half the world's steel and oil, and three-fourths of its cars and appliances. The whole world fears it and is baffled by it. Let U.S. industry slip 5 percent, and waves of apprehension sweep through foreign chancelleries [leaders]. Let U.S. consumer spending lag even half as much, and the most eminent economists anxiously read the omens. The whole world also marvels at and envies this market. It is enabling Americans to raise their standard of living every year while other countries have trouble in maintaining theirs. And of course the whole world wants to get in on it.*[4]

U.S. consumer spending is a large part of the nation's gross domestic product (GDP), or the value of all goods and services made within the country during a time period. The GDP is an indicator of the health of the U.S. economy. When spending slows, people fear the economy will suffer. Still, some critics point to American consumption as a driver of the depletion of natural resources. They also point to how some people jeopardize their economic security by falling into debt. Regardless of which side of this debate people fall on, all can agree that a robust economy could not have happened without the Industrial Revolution. Also, like the Industrial Revolution, a consumerist economy has its downsides as well as its advantages.

How You See History

1. Do radio and television still have influence over the American public? Why or why not?
2. Why do you think it took so much time for the airplane industry to succeed after the Wrights' flight?
3. Do you think modern American consumerism is positive or negative? Explain.

SYSTEM
CHANGE
NOT
CLIMATE
CHANGE!

CHAPTER SIX

FROM INDUSTRIAL TO HIGH-TECH

Today's world bears little resemblance to the world during the height of the Industrial Revolution. However, modern America owes its existence to pioneers such as Robert Fulton, Alexander Graham Bell, Henry Ford, and the Wright brothers. Many developments from the 19th and early 20th centuries are still vital to contemporary society. Cars and airplanes remain the most popular means of travel, though they are much more sophisticated. Telephones (and now smartphones) have become essential, and machine-oriented factories, refineries, and shipyards persist as centers of economic activity.

On the other hand, some U.S. industries that thrived during the Industrial Revolution are far less influential than they once were. Textile manufacturing, for example, takes place mainly in European and Asian countries, and email, phones, and other forms of communication have largely replaced the telegraph. Railroads, once the most important element in the country's quickly growing economy and geography, experienced a massive decline in passenger travel. These changes show that the U.S. economy is affected by technological, political, and cultural shifts. The face of business and industry continues to grow, change, and adapt, especially in the emergence of the Internet Age.

Alterations to Industry

American business at the beginning of the 21st century is different than it was a century ago. Industries are struggling with growing

In the modern world, societal pressure from the American public is pushing businesses to implement changes to combat climate change.

evidence that world supplies of coal and oil—the fuels of the Industrial Age—are being consumed at an unsustainable rate. This circumstance has led to the emergence of new industries devoted to alternative energy sources. Scientists have also linked industrial pollution and consumption of natural resources to climate change, species extinction, and other serious environmental problems. This knowledge has prompted heated debates on the best ways to balance economic growth and environmental protection. Many businesses have committed to practices or products that will reduce the amount of harmful gases released into the air, reuse materials that are difficult to break down in landfills, and better harness renewable sources of energy, such as solar and wind power.

Government regulation and oversight of businesses has also increased. It is often driven by concerns about workplace safety, fair treatment of employees, and financial security for workers who retire or get injured on the job. Industries sometimes fight back against what they consider restrictive regulations, claiming that they hinder businesses from operating as successfully as they could. However, many regulations are in place to protect both consumers and laborers.

The State of the Union

During the first half of the 20th century, unionization of the American workforce increased at a steady rate. At the height of the Great Depression in the mid-1930s, union membership stood at only 3 million members. General economic prosperity, talented and dedicated union leadership, and the support of powerful politicians such as Franklin D. Roosevelt later boosted the fortunes of labor organizations. By 1945, 15 million American workers held union memberships, largely in manufacturing industries, which was about 35 percent of all U.S. workers. However, since 1979, when the number of union workers reached a peak of 21 million, union membership has declined significantly. In 2019, union membership stood at 14.6 million workers, or 10.3 percent of the total workforce.

A leading factor in the decline of organized labor has been the steady shift of manufacturing jobs from American soil to foreign countries. Advances in transportation, communication, and other technological areas have enabled multinational corporations—businesses with offices in countries around the globe—to move their factories and other operations to countries where they can pay workers much lower wages. Environmental and workplace regulations are also less strict in many of these countries. In addition, international trade agreements have made it easier

Sometimes, workers use strikes to demand a change in their working conditions. Whether the issue is wages, safety, or health benefits, strikes interrupt production and force management to take notice.

for these same companies to ship foreign-made goods to the United States for sale. Finally, labor unions lost political power in many parts of the country in the 1980s, when pro-business politicians held growing influence in the White House and Congress.

These events have produced a remarkable drop in industrial manufacturing—the backbone of the Industrial Revolution—in the United States. Midcentury, manufacturing jobs accounted for 30 percent of all U.S. jobs. In 2019, just 8.5 percent of American jobs were in the manufacturing sector. During this period, jobs in the service industry—restaurants, retail stores, hotels, and other businesses that provide services rather than products—have increased. These service businesses, usually offering lower pay to their employees, also have lower unionization rates.

By the 21st century, 60 percent of all manufactured products sold in the United States were produced overseas. In 1960, that number was just 8 percent. This trend is present across nearly all industries—from toy manufacturing to automobile production. Many parts used in cars built in the United States actually come from factories in Mexico and other countries. Among suppliers of manufacturing technology and equipment, the drop in U.S. production is even more startling. According to the website IndustryWeek, U.S. machine tool manufacturers represented 28 percent of the world market in 1965, but in 2019, that number was just 5 percent. In 2018, American machine tool manufacturers exported $4.2 billion and imported $8.6 billion. Analysts believe that these trends are likely to continue.

Some think the U.S. manufacturing decline is not a cause for alarm because of the rise of American digital technology, including robotics, artificial intelligence, 3D printing, and other advances. Indeed, the global economy of the early 21st century has created opportunities for many such industries. Transportation, communications, and other high-tech industries have benefited enormously from scientific changes. The most spectacular growth has come in the computer and software industries. When commercial microprocessors—essentially, the brain of computers

PAST MEETS PRESENT: CHINA'S GROWTH AS AN ECONOMIC WORLD POWER

Since the 1990s, China has been undergoing what some economists call its Second Industrial Revolution. When Europe and the United States were building their industry-based economies, China had remained a nation based on agriculture. In the late 1900s, however, the Communist leadership of China decided to modernize its economy. Their policies, combined with a huge supply of labor and international trade agreements, have created an explosion of building in the nation's cities. Factories, shopping centers, and office buildings have sprouted up across China, and huge quantities of oil, iron ore, and other raw materials for manufacturers arrive at Chinese seaports every day. This economic growth has made China one of the greatest economic powers in the world.

In 2018, the trade deficit with China was $419 billion, with the United States importing $540 billion worth of goods and exporting $120 billion. That year, U.S. president Donald Trump attempted to reduce the enormous U.S. trade deficit partly by beginning a trade war with China. Trade wars begin when a nation places a kind of tax, called a tariff, or quotas on imported products. China responded to American tariffs in multiple ways: by refusing to buy certain U.S. goods, by imposing their own tariffs, and by agreeing to reduce other tariffs. In 2020, the two countries began to de-escalate the trade war. The effectiveness of trade wars is debated among economists. They can be costly to consumers who need to buy goods no matter where they come from, such as machine parts.

that are placed on silicon chips—were introduced into computers in the early 1970s, the computing power of these machines increased by leaps and bounds. In just a few years, computers became necessary for every large business enterprise. As historian John Steele Gordon noted, the computer could be compared to the steam engine in terms of its impact on the world:

> *The computer, like the steam engine, produced an economic revolution, and for precisely the same reason: it caused a collapse in the*

price of a fundamental input into the economic system, allowing that input to be applied to an infinity of tasks that previously had been too expensive or simply impossible. The steam engine brought down the price of work-doing energy; the computer brought down the price of storing, retrieving, and manipulating information.[1]

However, businesses making semiconductors and microprocessors, invented in the United States and so important to computers and other digital devices, have been moving their operations overseas for decades. Some trends will need to reverse for the United States to reclaim its manufacturing glory of the Industrial Revolution.

Entering the Internet Age

Computer and software industries owe much of their incredible growth and financial success to the internet. This vast global communications system of interconnected computer networks was built in the 1970s and 1980s by a community of scientists and entrepreneurs, including Tim Berners-Lee, Vinton Cerf, Robert Taylor, Robert Kahn, and Steve Case. In many ways, these and other early contributors to the internet were just as visionary as Henry Ford, Robert Fulton, and other legends of the Industrial Revolution. "The Internet … owed its exuberance and vigor to the spirit of entrepreneurs of all ages who can see a new, wide open, and limitless vista before them. The Internet is the new frontier,"[2] technology scholar Jeffrey Young wrote.

Since its emergence into general use in the early 1990s, the internet has completely changed the way people conduct business, communicate, and spend their free time. The changes to American business and industry in the Internet Age have been particularly dramatic. For example, computer technology has made it easier for businesses to interact with existing customers and attract new customers. Websites give companies the power to advertise products and services, communicate with clients, collect information about the use of their products, track inventory and shipping operations, and respond to customer feedback and changing tastes more quickly and efficiently.

Some U.S. industries have struggled to survive in this new information age. The recording industry, for example, has had to replace many of its old business practices to meet the demands of customers who have the capability of downloading digital recordings. Many record stores have been driven out of business by the changing environment.

THEY MADE HISTORY: VINTON CERF

Vinton Cerf was born on June 23, 1943, in New Haven, Connecticut. After graduating from Stanford University, he took a computer programming job with the technology company IBM. In the early 1970s, he moved on to the Advanced Research Projects Agency (ARPA), a division of the U.S. Department of Defense. At that time, the agency was working on the world's first computer network. This network, called ARPANET, is described as a forerunner of the internet.

During the 1970s, Cerf and his colleagues, including Robert Kahn, strung together a network of computers in locations across the country. In addition, they devised complex rules, or protocols, for network communication. They researched ways to connect the ARPANET to computer networks in Europe and elsewhere. These "internetworking" efforts became the basis for the term "internet."

Protocols introduced by Cerf and his fellow researchers became accepted in the late 1970s and early 1980s. Once computer scientists had these common rules, the development of a global computer network became an achievable goal. Cerf remained at the forefront of these efforts, and by the late 1980s, he was widely described as one of the "fathers" of the emerging internet.

Since that time, Cerf has remained involved in internet issues—from computing technology to governmental policy making. In 2004, he and Robert Kahn received the A. M. Turing Award in recognition of their essential role in the development of the internet. Cerf was awarded the Presidential Medal of Freedom in 2005. As of 2021, Cerf was serving as a vice president of the Google company.

However, the internet has paved the way for radio and streaming services like Spotify and Pandora, which offer ad-based and paid subscription streaming for access to their music libraries. In addition, independent musicians can promote and spread their music without a recording label, keeping more profits for themselves.

The internet has also been the breeding ground for major digital corporations, such as Amazon, Google, and Facebook, which have risen to become economic giants strictly on the basis of online sales and

HISTORY HAPPENED HERE: SILICON VALLEY

Silicon Valley is a region near San Francisco, California. Its name comes from the many electronics and computer companies that began there in the 20th and 21st centuries. (Silicon is a material used in the creation of semiconductors needed for computers.)

Some credit an educator named Frederick Terman for establishing the roots of Silicon Valley. As a teacher at California's Stanford University, he helped build the school into an esteemed research center, especially for radio and communications technology. He also encouraged talented engineering students to establish companies near the campus. In 1951, he helped launch the Stanford Industrial (now Research) Park, which leased university land to high-technology firms. These included some of the first technology "start-ups" and boasted such famous tenants as Eastman Kodak, Hewlett-Packard, and Lockheed.

In this photo, you can see the corporate headquarters of Apple, another giant of the digital age that established itself in Silicon Valley.

In 1959, there were about 18,000 high-technology jobs in Silicon Valley. Today, that number is over 436,000. Social media companies such as Facebook and LinkedIn are also based in Silicon Valley and have established new streams of revenue for technology firms.

advertisements. Countless smaller companies have carved out profitable positions for themselves as well. Furthermore, thousands of other retail and manufacturing companies have found ways to use the internet not only for online sales but also to boost revenue from traditional stores, shops, and manufacturing facilities.

Smartphone Innovations

Today, many have the internet at their disposal at every moment of the day, thanks to smartphones. People now have the ability to download

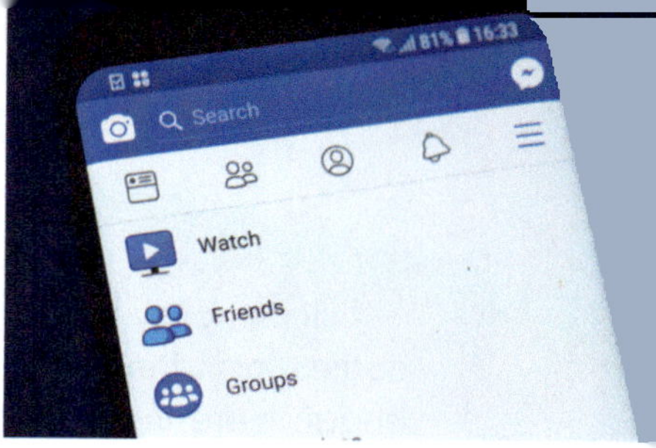

Companies like Facebook have continuously reinvented themselves and expanded their offerings to consumers—for example, offering digital entertainment—in order to increase profits.

applications, or apps, that play music and video and allow them to bank online, track diet and fitness goals, and connect with people around the world. Social media platforms—from Facebook to Twitter to Instagram—are catered to the smartphone market so people can stay linked. Companies such as Apple and Samsung market newer technologies, such as the smartwatch, that make daily life more tech-focused than just a few years ago.

With all the exciting innovations this technology has to offer, many wonder if society is becoming too dependent on virtual communication. A common criticism is that people spend too much time focusing on their devices and not enough time interacting face-to-face. Research has begun to study the effects of smartphones and other mobile digital devices on children. Early studies point to possible detrimental effects on children's social and emotional development when digital devices are the main method of distracting and calming young minds. However, increasingly, digital devices are being used in the classroom or to connect to the classroom for remote learning opportunities. Clearly, technology is here to stay for young and old alike.

Another concern about digital technology is the practice of sharing and selling people's private data. According to a 2019 Pew Research study, more than 80 percent of Americans say that they do not think they have control over data that companies collect online. Some of this data is used to market goods and services to people. Some is said to personalize online experiences, saving people time. However, many users do not trust what companies do with their private information. Only time will tell what ramifications these issues will have on Americans' lives in the years to come.

During the COVID-19 pandemic, children who could not attend school continued their academic studies through the use of digital technology.

FROM THE SOURCE: MARK ZUCKERBERG'S CONGRESSIONAL TESTIMONY

A grave concern about social media websites and applications is their toleration of misinformation. Some so-called "fake news" posts and messages are harmless. Others can have serious repercussions. Mark Zuckerberg, the CEO of Facebook, has been in the news repeatedly for discussions of what Facebook is doing to address misinformation. In a 2018 hearing before Congress, he apologized for Facebook's part in allowing Russian agents to interfere in the 2016 presidential election through social media as well as other misinformation campaigns:

> *It's clear now that we didn't do enough to prevent these [social media] tools from being used for harm as well. That goes for fake news, foreign interference in elections, and hate speech, as well as developers and data privacy. We didn't take a broad enough view of our responsibility, and that was a big mistake . . . It's not enough to just connect people, we have to make sure those connections are positive. It's not enough to just give people a voice, we have to make sure people aren't using it to hurt people or spread misinformation. It's not enough to give people control of their information, we have to make sure developers they've given it to are protecting it too. Across the board, we have a responsibility to not just build tools, but to make sure those tools are used for good.*[1]

During the COVID-19 pandemic, Facebook and Twitter were again called out for allowing misinformation about the virus to spread. Both companies continue to combat this issue with evolving policies and processes.

1. Quoted in Emily Stewart, "Mark Zuckerberg's Prepared Statement for Congressional Testimony," *Vox*, April 10, 2018, www.vox.com/policy-and-politics/2018/4/9/17215640/mark-zuckerberg-congress-testimony-facebook (accessed November 5, 2020).

What's Next?

Technological innovations are being introduced into business and society with stunning speed. So many of the tools used in daily life—including cars, computers, phones, cameras, televisions, household appliances, and home security systems—can be linked to networks that users can access from anywhere.

Many of the advancements to come will trace their lineage to the Industrial Revolution. No one can know the exact forms that American business and culture will take in the future. "We are watching something historic happen," wrote Microsoft founder Bill Gates in his book *The Road Ahead*, "and it will affect the world seismically, rocking us the same way the discovery of the scientific method, the invention of printing, and the arrival of the Industrial Age did."[3] As quickly as innovations appeared during the course of the Industrial Revolution, beginning with the steam engine, digital technology continues to make monumental changes to American—and global—society.

Today's technologically advanced global economy would never have come about if it had not been for inventions such as the steam engine, cotton gin, and telegraph. According to scholar Peter Stearns:

> *The final tally of the industrial revolution has yet to be reckoned ... The analysis is not simply a historical exercise, for the process is ongoing. The most fearsome toll of the industrial revolution may still await us in the form of greater environmental degradation or new kinds of conflicts between the haves and have-nots at the industrial table. Great opportunities may also beckon as various societies become increasingly able to make adjustments to the industrial world ... The industrial revolution, caused by an unusual set of circumstances in world history, unleashed forces that have been hard to control. The one certainty is that the process has not slowed. It continues to shape world history.*[4]

We are surrounded by the products and byproducts of the Industrial Age. Perhaps the Industrial Revolution's impact seems immeasurable because its effects have shaped our very lives.

How You See History

1. Do you think the decline of U.S. manufacturing is a problem? Why or why not?
2. What similarities do you see between the digital age and the Industrial Age?
3. Do you think the Industrial Age is over? Why or why not?

TIMELINE

1764
James Hargreaves invents the spinning jenny, the first successful spinning machine.

1765
Scottish inventor James Watt unveils a steam engine to power machinery.

1771
Richard Arkwright builds a cotton mill in England, an early example of the industrial factory system.

1793
Samuel Slater establishes the first successful cotton mill in the United States.

1794
Eli Whitney receives a patent for the cotton gin, creating an explosion of cotton production.

1807
Robert Fulton makes his famous steamboat journey up and down the Hudson River.

1825
The Erie Canal is completed, connecting the East Coast with the Midwest.

1834
Cyrus McCormick patents his mechanical reaper, transforming American farms.

1844
Samuel Morse sends the first message using his telegraph system.

1861
The American Civil War begins. Fighting continues until 1865.

1869
The first transcontinental railroad across the United States is completed.

1870
John D. Rockefeller forms the Standard Oil Company.

1876
Alexander Graham Bell files for a patent for his telephone.

1886
The American Federation of Labor, the most influential labor union in U.S. history, is founded.

1901
The U.S. Steel Corporation is established.

1903
The Wright brothers fly their motor-powered glider near Kitty Hawk, North Carolina.

1908
Henry Ford unveils the Model T automobile.

1925
Five million U.S. homes have radios.

1960
Ninety percent of U.S. homes have televisions.

1983
ARPANET adopts protocols that lead to the modern internet.

1992
The first smartphone is invented.

2014
Apple, Inc., introduces its first smartwatch.

NOTES

Introduction: A Revolution of Innovation

1. Peter N. Stearns, *The Industrial Revolution in World History* (Boulder, CO: Westview, 2007), p. 6.
2. Quoted in David Traxel, *Crusader Nation: The United States in Peace and the Great War: 1898–1920* (New York, NY: Knopf, 2006), p. 13.

Chapter One: Britain Sets the Stage

1. John Steele Gordon, *An Empire of Wealth: The Epic History of American Economic Power* (New York, NY: HarperCollins, 2004), pp. 88–89.
2. Quoted in Michael Burger, *The Shaping of Western Civilization: From Antiquity to the Present* (Toronto, ON: University of Toronto Press, 2013), p. 354.
3. Gordon, p. 84.
4. Quoted in Dale Anderson, *The Causes of the Civil War* (Milwaukee, WI: World Almanac Library, 2004), p. 8.
5. Stephen Yafa, *Cotton: The Biography of a Revolutionary Fiber* (New York, NY: Penguin, 2005), p. 72.

Chapter Two: America Takes the Lead

1. Quoted in Peter L. Bernstein, *Wedding of the Waters: The Erie Canal and the Making of a Great Nation* (New York, NY: Norton, 2005), p. 343.
2. Quoted in John Steele Gordon, *An Empire of Wealth: The Epic History of American Economic Power* (New York, NY: HarperCollins, 2004), p. 108.
3. Gordon, p. 141.
4. Gordon, p. 137.
5. Barbara Freese, *Coal: A Human History* (New York, NY: Basic Books, 2003), p. 121.
6. Quoted in Robert J. Samuelson, "Republic of Turmoil," *Washington Post*, November 24, 2004, www.washingtonpost.com/archive/opinions/2004/11/24/republic-of-turmoil/.

Chapter Three: An Economic Power Emerges

1. Quoted in David H. Bain, "For All the Human Family," *New York Times*, archive.nytimes.com/www.nytimes.com/books/first/b/bain-empire.html (accessed October 2, 2020).
2. *Putnam's Monthly*, "Statistics and Speculations Concerning the Pacific Railroad," September 1853, p. 271.
3. James Howard Bridge, *The Carnegie Millions and the Men Who Made Them* (London, UK: Limpus, Baker & Co., 1903), p. 169.
4. John Steele Gordon, *An Empire of Wealth: The Epic History of American Economic Power* (New York, NY: HarperCollins, 2004), p. 149.
5. Gordon, p. 153.

Chapter Four: Transformed by Industry

1. Stuart Bruchey, *Enterprise: The Dynamic Economy of a Free People* (Cambridge, MA: Harvard University Press, 1990), p. 363.
2. Michael McGerr, *A Fierce Discontent: The Rise and Fall of the Progressive Movement in America* (New York, NY: Free Press, 2003), pp. 151–152.
3. Theodore Roosevelt, "First Annual Message," The American Presidency Project, www.presidency.ucsb.edu/documents/first-annual-message-16 (accessed October 4, 2020).
4. John Steele Gordon, *An Empire of Wealth: The Epic History of American Economic Power* (New York, NY: HarperCollins, 2004), p. 166.

Chapter Five: New Developments in the 1900s

1. Claude S. Fischer, *America Calling: A Social History of the Telephone to 1940* (Berkeley, CA: University of California Press, 1992), p. 34.
2. Robert L. Hilliard and Michael C. Keith, *The Broadcast Century and Beyond: A Biography of American Broadcasting* (New York, NY: Focal, 2001), pp. 23–24.
3. Joann Muller, Kathleen Kerwin, and David Welch, "Autos: A New Industry," *Bloomberg*, July 15, 2002, www.bloomberg.com/news/articles/2002-07-14/autos-a-new-industry.
4. Quoted in David M. Kennedy and Thomas Bailey, *The American Spirit: U.S. History as Seen by Contemporaries*, vol. II (Boston, MA: Wadsworth, 2010), p. 481.

Chapter Six: From Industrial to High-Tech

1. John Steele Gordon, *An Empire of Wealth: The Epic History of American Economic Power* (New York, NY: HarperCollins, 2004), p. 409.
2. Quoted in Robert Sobel, *The Great Boom 1950–2000: How a Generation of Americans Created the World's Most Prosperous Society* (New York, NY: St. Martin's, 2016), PDF e-book.
3. *Buffalo News*, "Bill Gates' Brave New World," December 15, 1995, buffalonews.com/news/bill-gates-brave-new-world/article_addc9536-42a5-533b-8546-56b7ccd99646.html.
4. Peter N. Stearns, *The Industrial Revolution in World History* (New York, NY: Routledge, 2018), e-book.

FOR MORE INFORMATION

Books: Nonfiction

Hahn, Barbara. *Technology in the Industrial Revolution*. Cambridge, UK: Cambridge University Press, 2020.

Helfand, Lewis. *The Industrial Revolution*. New Delhi, India: Campfire, 2017.

Uhl, Xina M., and Corona Brezina. *A Primary Source Investigation of the Industrial Revolution*. New York, NY: Rosen Publishing Group, 2019.

Books: Fiction

Canasi, Brittany. *Not on My Watch*. Vero Beach, FL: Rourke Educational Media, 2017.

Gilbert, Julie. *Lucy Fights the Flames: A Triangle Shirtwaist Factory Survival Story*. North Mankato, MN: Stone Arch Books, 2020.

Kim, Gyeong-hwa. *Leather Shoe Charlie*. Grand Rapids, MI: Eerdmans Books for Young Readers, 2017.

Websites

Erie Canalway National Heritage Corridor

eriecanalway.org/

Learn more about the history of the Erie Canal, explore sites along the canal, and discover places where you can enjoy hiking, kayaking, and sightseeing.

The Industrial Revolution

www.khanacademy.org/humanities/big-history-project/acceleration/bhp-acceleration/a/the-industrial-revolution

Read about the rise and spread of the Industrial Age, beginning with what happened in Great Britain.

The Industrial Revolution

www.nationalgeographic.org/topics/resource-library-industrial-revolution/

Check out enlightening links about this time period through the *National Geographic* website.

Sir Richard Arkwright's Cromford Mills

www.cromfordmills.org.uk/

This website, maintained by the Arkwright Society, includes historical information, photographs, videos, and much more.

INDEX

PHOTO CREDITS

Cover Photo Josse/Leemage/Contributor/Corbis Historical/Getty Images; pp. 4, 34 Universal History Archive/Contributor/Universal Images Group/Getty Images; p. 6 MPI/Stringer/Archive Photos/Getty Images; pp. 10, 14 Science & Society Picture Library/Contributor/SSPL/Getty Images; pp. 15, 24 Chronicle/Alamy Stock Photo; pp. 16, 37, 52 Print Collector/Contributor/Hulton Archive/Getty Images; p. 17 Cvijovic Zarko/Shutterstock.com; p. 18 World History Archive/Alamy Stock Photo; pp. 19, 54 Photo 12/Contributor/Universal Images Group/Getty Images; p. 21 American Stock Archive/Contributor/Archive Photos/Getty Images; p. 27 The Protected Art Archive/Alamy Stock Photo; pp. 28 (top), 32, 60, 73, 79 Bettmann/Contributor/Bettmann/Getty Images; p. 28 (bottom) Spiroview Inc/Shutterstock.com; p. 31 DEA PICTURE LIBRARY/Contributor/De Agostini/Getty Images; p. 38 Otto Herschan Collection/Stringer/Hulton Archive/Getty Images; p. 41 Courtesy of the Library of Congress Prints and Photographs Division; p. 43 Weldon Schloneger/Shutterstock.com; p. 44 Courtesy of the Library of Congress Geography and Map Division; p. 45 Ed Vebell/Contributor/Archive Photos/Getty Images; pp. 47, 50 Stock Montage/Contributor/Archive Photos/Getty Images; p. 58 BC Images/Shutterstock.com; pp. 63, 77 Hulton Deutsch/Contributor/Corbis Historical/Getty Images; p. 65 Everett Collection/Shutterstock.com; p. 66 Underwood Archives/Contributor/Archive Photos/Getty Images; p. 68 Mark Goebel Photo Gallery/Contributor/Archive Photos/Getty Images; p. 71 PhotoQuest/Contributor/Archive Photos/Getty Images; p. 75 Mondadori Portfolio/Contributor/Mondadori Portfolio/Getty Images; p. 82 DisobeyArt/Shutterstock.com; p. 85 Lambert/Contributor/Archive Photos/Getty Images; p. 89 JHVEPhoto/Shutterstock.com; p. 90 (top) Grey82/Shutterstock.com; p. 90 (bottom) Travelpixs/Shutterstock.com.

ABOUT THE AUTHOR

Therese Harasymiw has written and edited more than 300 nonfiction books for children and teens, including works on technology, engineering, and entrepreneurs of the Industrial Revolution. Harasymiw received an English degree from Providence College and a master of education degree in English education from the State University of New York at Buffalo. A former high school literature teacher, she works as an editor in educational publishing. Harasymiw and her family reside in Rochester, New York.